I0605753

KAPUSTA

ALISSA TIMOSHKINA

KAPUSTA

VEGETABLE-FORWARD RECIPES FROM EASTERN EUROPE

PHOTOGRAPHY BY LAURA EDWARDS

quadrille

ALISSA TIMOSHKINA

One

CABBAGE

Two

BEETROOT

Three

POTATO

Four

DUMPLINGS

Five

CARROT

Six

MUSHROOMS

Seven

PICKLES AND FERMENTS

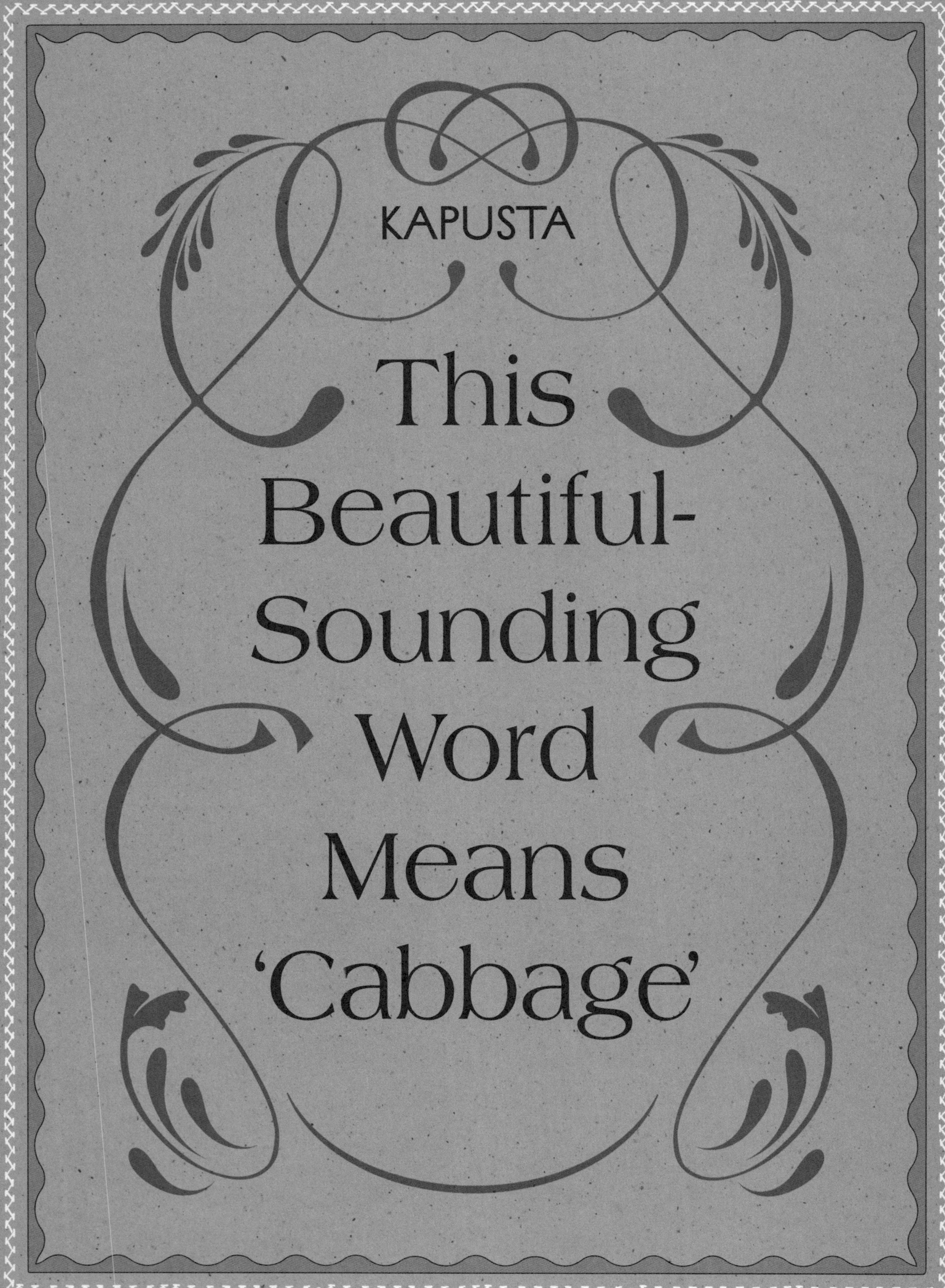

KAPUSTA

This Beautiful-Sounding Word Means 'Cabbage'

Introduction

Kapusta. This beautiful-sounding word means 'cabbage' in many Eastern European Slavic languages, including Belarusian, Polish, Russian, Slovak and Ukrainian. To me, the vegetable represents simple and nourishing home food. Its scents and flavours weave through the fabric of my childhood memories. Kapusta also symbolises my personal creative journey as a cook, both at home and professionally. When I used to spend my summers in various language schools in England during the early 1990s, I would sometimes be faced with a well-meaning but slightly condescending remark: 'Oh, all you eat over there is cabbage!' With 'there' denoting any Eastern European country from behind the notorious Iron Curtain. Indeed, this is a stereotype rooted in the dreadful reality of life under the socialist dictatorship, most memorably depicted by George Orwell in the opening of his novel *1984* (ironically, this is the year I was born): 'It was a bright cold day in April, and the clocks were striking thirteen. Winston Smith, his chin nuzzled into his breast in an effort to escape the vile wind, slipped quickly through the glass doors of Victory Mansions, though not quickly enough to prevent a swirl of gritty dust from entering along with him. The hallway smelt of boiled cabbage and old rag mats.' This stark scene of dystopian reality is set so precisely, where the scent of cabbage symbolises the bleak oppressive regime itself.

While I was initially haunted by this stereotype, when I came to cook and write about food professionally in London in the mid-2010s, I was determined to turn this cliché onto its head, and empower myself with the ancestral knowledge of how to cook well with cabbage. I reached into the treasure chest of my childhood food memories and saw plump savoury buns stuffed with cabbage and mushrooms, zingy, fresh cabbage salads dressed in unrefined sunflower seed oil, comforting soups and stews of sour cabbage and grains, and, of course, the most important, formative food-memory of all – the sauerkraut; its tang, its crunch, and the ritual of preparing it!

Coincidentally, this was happening at a time when the Western food scene was starting to discover a new food trend – fermentation. Us folk in Eastern Europe have been fermenting for centuries and pickles and ferments are something we consider to be slightly 'boring' (yet much-loved) food staples.

Now that the world was ready for cabbage, I was ready to spread the cabbage gospel far and wide. Having written *Salt & Time*, in 2019, a title inspired by the process of fermentation, I was toying with the idea of writing a follow-up book entirely dedicated to her majesty the cabbage. However, eventually, cabbage became a symbol of Eastern European vegetable-forward cooking in my mind. And that's what this book is all about: simple, nutrient-rich, veg-centric cooking, which could only have emerged in the part of the world that is notorious for its political turmoils, on the one hand, and yet is also blessed with the most biodiverse and rich landscapes, on the other. At the core of this cuisine (if you pardon the cabbage pun) lay a profound respect and reverence towards food, cultivated over the centuries. And this is what makes the Eastern European way of cooking and eating so relevant today! Here in the West issues of food waste and the accompanying environmental crisis forced us to reconsider our attitudes towards food, finally bringing seasonal, humble vegetable-forward cooking to the heart of many kitchens. So here, it turns out, we also need a little more of that kapusta mindset in our homes.

In this book I focus on the top five most popular vegetables in Eastern Europe – starting with cabbage, followed by beetroot, potato, carrot and mushrooms – and tap in to seasonal, sustainable and low-cost eating, a tendency that is at the fore of the current food discourse. Holding the magnificent five (vegetables) at its heart, the book also features an array of herbs and spices, invites a bounty of other vegetables onto your kitchen counter, and offers a handful of meat recipes, which can be easily adapted for a vegetarian diet.

In each chapter, you will find a diversity of dishes, from dips and salads, to soups, stews and mains, as well as some desserts, to surprise your palette. Since dumplings and ferments form such a huge part of the Eastern European culinary DNA, I wanted to give them both a dedicated chapter, with all five vegetables shining brightly in each.

I have always believed that food is a form of a conversation between people – between the generations of the same family, or between the members of local and global communities. And I see these five vegetables as key elements of our culinary vocabulary, which remind us that food is indeed a common language we all speak. Despite so many (imposed) differences between groups of people, food has always proven to be the language of unity. It is my hope that by celebrating a handful of humble vegetables this book will shine the spotlight on a whole kaleidoscope of little-known culinary cultures and histories from Eastern Europe, reminding us that we have far more in common than what holds us apart.

A Culinary Melting Pot at the Crossroads of History

Defining Eastern Europe

Europe was born in ancient Greece as a concept in the minds of the great philosophers. Since then, its meaning, location and role in the world has kept evolving. The understanding that there are two parts to the European continent, the Western and the Eastern, was not formed overnight, but nevertheless can be traced back to the era of Charlemagne aka Charles the Great (AD 747–814), when a symbolic line was drawn down from the river Elbe. This tentative geographic divide developed due to religious and linguistic differences between the Western and the Eastern branches of Christianity, under the influences of the Roman (Latin) and the Byzantine (Greek) churches and languages, respectively. Both the West and the East, as well as their neighbours outside the European continent, played an active part in shaping and defining their identities against one another, thus gradually building the concept of Eastern Europe we know today. This process continued over the centuries, with the rise and fall of numerous empires, as well as in the aftermath of the two world wars. World War II was also responsible for the creation of the notorious 'Eastern' or 'Socialist bloc' – a traumatic period of Communist rule over a vast area of Eastern, South-Eastern and Central Europe from 1945 to the late 1980s/early 1990s. Its history became a stigma that got stuck to the countries of that region long after the political union itself collapsed.

While there are various ways to define Eastern Europe, with some lists featuring the Baltics, the Balkans and even the Caucasus, reminding us that the term is nothing but a socio-political and cultural construct, in this book I have decided to rely on the UN's current definition which, at the time of writing in 2023, included Belarus, Bulgaria, the Czech Republic, Hungary, Moldova, Poland, Romania, Slovakia, Ukraine and the western part of Russia. However, I will allow myself a personal choice to limit references to Russia. Living in a post-24/02/22 world, I simply cannot bring myself to celebrate the culinary culture of the country (despite having been born there) that has launched an atrocious war in the heart of Eastern Europe, in Ukraine. However, while refraining from using an umbrella term 'Russian cuisine', I do want to give a voice to the indigenous ethnic groups residing in the Eastern European part of the country, such as the Volga Tatars and the Udmurts, whose little-known culinary culture deserves our attention.

Ukrainian cuisine, of course, plays a big part in this book, and the history of the country itself can be appreciated as a microcosm of the entire Eastern Europe, a buffer zone between the West and the East with frequently shifting borders. While for many this historical specificity of the Eastern European region has led to associations with 'poverty', 'lack of freedom', 'food shortages', 'uniformity' and 'oppression', to me the fact that Eastern Europe withstood the conquests and saw the fall of many once-powerful empires, from the Roman to the Soviet, raising up each time with a renewed sense of pride and value of ones origin and history, speaks of courage, resourcefulness, endurance and freedom. And this is something that is intricately reflected in the cuisine of the region.

DENMARK
BALTIC
SEA
Warsaw
POLAND
GERMANY
Prague
CZECH REPUBLIC
SLOVAKIA
Vienna
Bratislava
AUSTRIA
Budapest
HUNGARY
SWITZERLAND
SLOVENIA
Ljubljana
Zagreb
CROATIA
ITALY
BOSNIA
AND
HERCEGOVINA
Belgrade
SERBIA
Sarajevo
MONTENEGRO
Podgorica
Pristina
KOSOVO
Skopje
MACEDONIA
Tirana
ALBANIA

LATVIA
Moscow
Minsk
BELARUS
RUSSIA
Kyiv
UKRAINE
MOLDOVA
Chisinau
SEA OF AZOV
Bucharest
BLACK SEA
TURKEY
Ankara

Defining Eastern European Cuisine

While throughout its long history, a lot of damage has been done to the indigenous traditions of Eastern European regions by the invading powers, most recently by the stifling Socialist regime and its dogma of uniformity, each country remains as diverse as its own regions – linguistically, religiously, culturally and gastronomically. What's more, since the dawn of time, the geographical position of the region, with its abundance of rivers, forests, mountains and plains, made it the perfect highway for explorers, traders, invaders and settlers, and so produced a cultural and hence culinary landscape of extraordinary variety, ranging as far and wide as the Slavs, the Romans, the Greeks, the Bulgars, the Tatar-Mongols, the Ottomans, the Austro-Hungarians, the Roma and the Ashkenazi Jews. No other part of Europe can boast such a cornucopia of histories and flavours.

The cuisine of Eastern Europe is so regionally diverse that in some places the bordering countries have more in common between them than the distant regions within the same country. A rich tapestry of historical events created a group of cuisines that is in constant dialogue with one another, remembering its shared past and contemplating the global tendencies of its future.

Although it is impossible to offer an exhaustive list of all types of dishes common in Eastern European cuisines, I have grouped together the most common meals, cooking techniques, ingredients and spices in the hope of giving you an inviting glimpse of the recipes to expect in this book.

• Chunky soups and stews with grains and vegetables (cabbage, sauerkraut, mushrooms, carrots, potatoes and beetroot).

• Dumplings of all shapes and sizes, filled with cabbage, potatoes, mushrooms and grains, as well as curd cheese, plums and summer berries.

• Plump pastries and pies filled with moreish ingredients from mashed potatoes, to sauerkraut, mushrooms, crumbly cheeses and fresh berries, which go by the names of pyrizhky, knishes, placinte, vertuta, and banitsa, to name just a few.

• Fermented food is a real pillar of the region's cuisine. Lacto-fermented grains, fruits and vegetables give a distinct complexity and a satisfying tang to so many dishes.

• Cabbage rolls with meat or veggie fillings often poached in a tomato and/or sour cream sauce: sarmale in Romania, sarma in Bulgaria, golabki in Poland and holubtsi in Ukraine, the list goes on.

• The smoky flavour of paprika is a staple, and so are the flavours of sweet and nutty caraway and coriander seeds, fragrant fennel seeds and fresh or dried dill, and warming black pepper.

• An abundance of sour cream and fresh green herbs (dill and parsley) as a topping for many soups, stews, dumplings and pancakes.

Hearty, nourishing, bursting with simple but powerful flavours of local produce, seasonal and always soulful, the cuisine of the vast region of Eastern Europe holds so much culinary wonder that I simply can't wait to explore it with you.

CABBAGE

CHAPTER ONE

CABBAGE

Cabbage is a wonder-vegetable! It has been on the tables of humans from ancient times and has been a firm staple in Eastern Europe since the 16th century. A loyal companion of *Homo sapiens*, cabbage is relatively easy to grow in a variety of climates and it can keep for a long time after harvesting, which makes it the perfect vegetable for the Eastern European climate, both meteorological and political. It is bursting with nutrients in its fresh and fermented forms, often helping to restore nutritional balance during times of hardships, of which there were plenty in the region throughout history. Perhaps its life-saving property explains the old myth of babies coming out of cabbages, as if the vegetable itself is potent enough to give life. Eating cabbage as well as placing softened cabbage leaves on a young-mother's breasts was believed to increase milk supply, too.

Indeed, cabbage is mind-blowing in its versatility – it has as many culinary uses as the gorgeous venous leaves that make up its globe-like body. Eat it fresh with plenty of salt and fragrant oil, use its leaves to encase juicy fillings or turn them into flavourful fillings for pies, stew it in soups, fry it, roast it or preserve it with salt to make the marvellous sauerkraut. I offer recipes for all of these here.

White Cabbage Slaw with Carrots, Peppers and Sunflower Seeds

This salad sings the story of an Eastern European spring on the cusp of summer. Bursting with simple ingredients, it creates a symphony of surprisingly complex flavours and satisfying textures – crunchy, juicy, sweet, tart, tangy, nutty, floral and herbaceous. Try this as a side to a barbecue, as part of a mezze-style spread of dips and salads, or add it into a cheese and charcuterie sandwich. Whichever way you eat it, this salad will become a staple on your table. Feel free to omit the currants or swap them for dried cranberries. I recommend using top-quality unrefined sunflower oil, though a premium rapeseed oil would work equally well.

Serves
4–6

½ medium white cabbage, roughly 450g (1lb)

1 sweet and tart apple, cored

1 red or yellow (bell) pepper, cored and deseeded

1 large carrot, peeled and grated

large bunch of dill, fronds and stalks, finely chopped

2 tablespoons sunflower seeds, toasted, plus extra to serve

handful of red currants or dried cranberries

FOR THE DRESSING

zest and juice of ½ lemon

2 tablespoons apple cider vinegar

1 teaspoon runny honey (or a pinch of sugar)

4 tablespoons quality unrefined sunflower oil

flaky sea salt to taste

Start by thinly slicing all the vegetables (apart from the carrot) using a mandoline. Although highly precarious, this method results in evenly sliced vegetables, which allows them to absorb the dressing in equal measure and creates a delightful sensory experience in your mouth.

Place the vegetables in a large mixing bowl and season with a big pinch of salt.

To make the dressing, mix all the ingredients in a separate bowl and give them a whisk. Taste and adjust to your liking – add more salt or balance out the sweetness and acidity.

Pour the dressing over the vegetables and give them a gentle massage with your hands.

Next, add the dill, sunflower seeds and red currants. Gently toss, then serve.

If you like, add another pinch of salt, and scatter over more dill, currants and seeds.

Cabbage, Pea and Dill Fritters

Fritters are an entire culinary genre in Eastern European cuisine. Quick and simple to make, they require no more than a handful of basic ingredients while providing flavour, sustenance and comfort. A whole range of (root) vegetables can be used to make a fritter; potato, beetroot, carrot and courgette (zucchini) being the most popular. Cabbage, albeit less of a top contender, is by far my favourite. Whatever the vegetable you choose, the one thing you must enjoy (aside from the uber-satisfying golden crunch) is a side of cooling sour cream for dipping!

Makes
10 (APPROX)

- 100g (¾ cup) frozen peas
- ½ medium white cabbage, weighing approx. 450g (1lb)
- ½ tablespoon fine salt, plus extra to taste
- 3–4 spring onions (scallions)
- 1 medium bunch of dill
- 2 eggs
- 4 tablespoons plain (all-purpose) flour, plus extra if needed
- vegetable oil, for shallow frying
- sour cream, to serve

Start by defrosting the peas by submerging them in boiled water.

Finely shred the cabbage on a mandoline (or thinly slice), put into a bowl with the fine salt and let it sit while you finely chop the spring onions and the dill.

Massage the cabbage a little with your hands, until most of the juices are released. Strain, squeezing out as much liquid as possible, and return to the bowl together with the spring onions and dill.

Drain the peas and add them to the same bowl.

In a separate bowl, whisk the eggs with a pinch of salt and stir in the flour to create the batter.

Pour the batter into the larger bowl with the vegetables and mix well, with a fork. If the mix is too runny, add another tablespoon of flour.

Heat enough oil in a frying pan for shallow frying (4–6 tablespoons, depending on the size of your pan).

Using your hands, form around 1½ heaped tablespoons of the mixture in to a fritter shape, and shallow-fry for 5–6 minutes on each side over a medium heat, until golden and crisp.

Remove and let cool on paper towel to absorb excess oil, then serve with some sour cream while hot or at room temperature.

Piroshki Buns with Cabbage, Spring Onion and Hard-Boiled Eggs

Humans must be genetically wired to fall helplessly in love with any foodstuff that gives us the joy biting into a crispy yet pillowy dough and discovering a juicy filling inside. *Piroshki* are a brilliant example of that. An Eastern European equivalent of Asian samosas or Latin American empanadas, these oblong-shaped wonders are made with leavened dough (yes!) and most often shallow-fried in oil (yes please!). When it comes to fillings, the possibilities are endless. The classic filling is cabbage. Also common is hard-boiled egg and spring onion. Here I frivolously mix those two together. You'll find *piroshki* filled with peppery mashed potatoes too, or braised sauerkraut with mushrooms, not to mention jams and stewed apples.

The origin of *piroshki* is commonly believed to be ancient Russia. The word itself – pronounced as *pirozhki* – is a diminutive of *pirog* (a pie), which in turn originates from *pir*, Russian for 'feast'. However, having dug around, I've come to the conclusion that the history of this delightful dish is tainted by the prevailing confusion between ancient Russia and ancient Rus'. Rus' was an Eastern Slavic political entity (9th–13th centuries) that predated Russia and encompassed the territory of modern day Ukraine, Belarus, parts of the Baltics and parts of Western Russia, with its capital in Kyiv; hence its alternative name – Kyivan Rus'. So the origins of this dish can be equally attributed to Ukraine, or Belarus, where it is indeed a staple to this day and the etymology of the word follows the same logic – *pyrizhky*, *pyrig*, *pyr* in Ukrainian.

The global popularity of this dish, albeit under an easier to pronounce misnomer, *piroshki*, is astonishing: from Greece and Iran to Japan and the United States. And rightly so! Try it and you will see why.

Makes
20–25

1 teaspoon dried yeast

50ml (1¾fl oz/3½ tablespoons) warm water

1 teaspoon sugar

250ml (8fl oz/1 cup) warm milk

1 egg

1 teaspoon salt

1 tablespoon vegetable oil

500g (1lb 2oz) plain (all-purpose) flour, plus more for dusting

To make the dough, mix the dried yeast, warm water, sugar and 50 ml (1¾fl oz/3½ tablespoons) of milk in a cup, and let it rest in a warm place for 5–10 minutes or until the mixture starts to bubble. In a large bowl whisk together the rest of the milk, egg, salt, oil and the yeast mixture until you get a smooth frothy liquid.

Start adding the flour in batches, whisking constantly to ensure there are no lumps. Once the whisk starts getting stuck in the dough, continue mixing with your hands. Eventually the dough should stop sticking to your hands. But if not, you can always add more flour at a later stage. Once you have incorporated all the flour, cover the bowl with clingfilm and let it rest for 1 hour or until it has doubled in size. In the meantime, prepare the filling.

Heat the oil in a large frying pan or a casserole (Dutch oven). Fry the cabbage with the spring onion, stirring occasionally over medium heat for 10–15 minutes, until still crunchy but slightly caramelised.

FOR THE FILLING

vegetable oil, for shallow frying

500g (1lb 2oz) white cabbage, thinly shredded

1 medium bunch of spring onions (scallions), thinly sliced

100g (3½oz) salted butter

1 bunch of dill, finely chopped

4 eggs, hard-boiled

salt and black pepper

Take off the heat, add the butter, the dill and the chopped hard-boiled eggs, and season generously with salt and black pepper. Let it cool down.

Now, let's get back to the dough. Once it has doubled in size, tip it out onto a work surface generously dusted with flour. Divide the dough in half and cover one half with a tea towel or a cling film to prevent it from drying while you knead the other. Work the dough for a few minutes, adding more flour, if needed, as you go along.

Divide the dough into small chunks, around 45g (1½oz) each, and pat them out into round discs 8–10cm (3¼–4in) in diameter. Add 2 tablespoons of filling to each disc and seal the edges by lifting them towards the middle. Try to distribute the filling as evenly throughout as you can. Flatten each bun slightly, lay them out on a dusted tray or parchment paper and cover with cling film, while you finish the rest.

To fry the buns, set a frying pan over a medium heat and heat enough oil for shallow-frying (4–6 tablespoons, depending on the size of your pan; you might need to keep adding more as the buns will absorb a lot). Fry the buns in small batches (3–4) on each side for 3 minutes. Remove and let rest on some paper towels to absorb excess oil, then serve immediately with some black tea with honey and lemon.

Polish Kapusniak Soup

Among the myriad of dishes that Eastern Europeans have come up with for cabbage, soups are an indisputable classic, and a real culinary signature of the region. And what can represent this category better than the gorgeous Polish *kapusniak* soup (literally meaning 'a cabbage soup'). Very similar to its Russian counterpart *shchi,* in my view, the Polish soup benefits from the smokiness and the richness of the kielbasa (a kind of Polish chorizo). You can make a vegan version too; simply omit the sausage and use more wild mushrooms instead. Flavoured with sweet marjoram and caraway seeds, the complexity of the dish is maximised by its star ingredient, the mighty cabbage, or rather its fermented incarnation – sauerkraut. Sour, tangy, smoky and sweet! Can you think of a better flavour profile?

Serves
4–6

200g (7oz) Polish kielbasa, cut into bite-sized chunks

vegetable oil, for frying (optional)

1 onion, thinly sliced

2 carrots, peeled and grated

2 tablespoons dried marjoram

1 teaspooon caraway seeds

50g (1¾oz) dried wild mushrooms, soaked, drained and roughly chopped

2 litres (68fl oz/8 cups) beef stock

2 bay leaves

2 potatoes, peeled and diced

300g (10½oz) Classic Sauerkraut (see page 184) or shop-bought sauerkraut

2 tablespoons finely chopped dill, plus extra to garnish

salt and black pepper to taste

sour cream, to serve (optional)

chopped parsley, to serve

Heat a large, heavy-based lidded pan or casserole (Dutch oven) over a medium heat.

Add the kielbasa and fry for 8 minutes. The meat will most likely release enough fat to fry the vegetable For the pie s, but if not, you can add a small drizzle of oil.

Next, add the onion and carrots along with a pinch of salt, giving them a thorough mix to coat in the lovely kielbasa fat. Cover with a lid and fry for 10 minutes, stirring occasionally.

Add the marjoram and the caraway seeds. If using mushrooms, add them next. Pour in the stock, add the bay leaves and the potatoes, then bring to boil and cook until the potatoes are tender.

Next, add the sauerkraut together with its brine and the dill. Bring to a simmer, take off the heat, cover with the lid and let it rest for 1 hour.

When ready to eat, serve the soup hot with a dollop of sour cream, if you like, and a generous sprinkling of fresh dill and some black pepper.

Czech Kyselica Soup

Eastern European cuisine is known for its affinity with sour flavours, and when it comes to soups of the region we find ourselves in the Kingdom of Sour. Most often the effect is achieved by adding fermented cabbage or other fermented vegetables, such as the Polish *kapusniak* or *zoupa ogórkowa*, or the Ukrainian borsch varieties with sauerkraut, but there are also soups that use fermented wheat or rye starters, like the Romanian *barś*, the Polish and Belarussian *zurek* or the Russian *okroshka* with *kvass*. The Czech Republic has an entire collection of their own sour soups: *zelňačka*, *kyselica*, *kyselo* and *kulajda*. The sourness of this soup is taken to the next level with the addition of sour cream to the sauerkraut broth. Although this might seem like an overwhelming emphasis on one flavour, the sour cream adds a very pleasant sweet and velvety undertone. While the original old Wallachian recipe for *kyselica* also contains pancetta, butter, milk and flour, I have decided to take pity on our pancreases, and have created a much lighter vegetarian version, not compromising on the *kyselo* (sour) quality, of course!

Serves
4

- vegetable oil, for frying
- 1 onion, thinly sliced
- 1 carrot, peeled and grated
- 1 teaspoon caraway seeds
- 500g (1lb 2oz) chestnut mushrooms, chopped
- 1.5 litres (51fl oz/6 cups) vegetable stock
- 4 potatoes, peeled and diced
- 4 bay leaves
- 6 allspice berries
- 250g (9oz) Classic sauerkraut (see page 184) or shop-bought
- 250g (9oz) sour cream
- 1 small bunch of parsley, finely chopped
- salt and black pepper, to taste

Heat some oil in a larg For the pie e lidded saucepan and fry the onion and carrots with a pinch of salt for 8 minutes. Stir through the caraway seeds and let it fry for another couple of minutes.

Add the mushrooms to the pan, along with another pinch of salt. Fry for 5 minutes, or until the juices from the mushrooms are released.

Add the stock, potatoes, bay leaves and the allspice berries, bring to boil and simmer for 10–15 minutes, until the potatoes are cooked through.

Take off the heat, add the sauerkraut and the sour cream, cover with the lid and let the soup rest for a few hours (if you have time).

When ready to serve, warm up the soup (if necessary), sprinkle over the parsley, adjust the seasoning and be prepared to travel to sour-central!

A Cabbage Strudel

Eastern European cuisine is built of lucious savoury pies of all shapes and sizes. The pastry of these pies can tell you a lot about the intricate culinary history of the particular area within the region. While leavened dough, such as in the *piroshki* buns (page 30) is used widely, the influence of the former Ottoman Empire is particularly prominent in the southern regions where we find borek-like *placinta* (Romania), *vertuta* (Moldova), or *banitsa* (Bulgaria) made with hand-stretched filo pastry. The name strudel, of course, immediately nods to the Austro-Hungarian Empire, though some sources suggest that the pastry was in fact born out of the Ottoman rule too.

While we all know (and adore) sweet strudels, a cabbage one is a lesser-known staple within the Ashkenazi Hungarian community, where it is known as *káposztás rétes.*

This pie is particularly popular during the Jewish Purim holiday as cabbage is thought to soften the impact of the long alcohol-fuelled festivities. This pie is a show stopper meal for 10–12, you can either make two small pies or halve all the ingredients to serve 4–6.

Serves
10–12

olive oil, for frying

2 onions, thinly sliced

1 teaspoon caraway seeds (optional)

800g (1lb 12oz) white cabbage, thinly shredded

splash of white wine

150g (5½oz) salted butter

1 small bunch of dill, finely chopped

salt and black pepper to taste (I'd recommend being generous with both)

garlic yoghurt sauce (see page 124), to serve

FOR THE PIE

1 packet of ready-to-use filo pastry (270–300g/9½–10½oz/ 7–8 sheets)

100g (3½oz) melted butter

Heat the oil in a lidded pan and fry the onions with a pinch of salt for 8–10 minutes, until translucent and slightly caramelised. Add the caraway seeds, if using, and give it a thorough stir.

Add the cabbage with another pinch of salt, stir thoroughly and cook for 10 minutes. Add the wine, turn the heat to high and let the alcohol bubble and evaporate. Lower the heat to medium, cover with the lid, and cook for another 8 minutes. Add the 150g (5½oz) of butter and the dill, stir through and take off the heat. Let it cool a little.

Preheat the oven to 200°C (400°F).

To shape the strudel, lay out a sheet of filo pastry on top of a sheet of paper towel or parchment paper, shortest side towards you, and brush generously with the butter, then top with another sheet. Repeat with two more sheets (you will need four in total).

Place half of the cabbage filling in a 5cm (2in) thick log parallel to the short edge of the pasty about 2cm (¾in) away from the edge. Then, using the paper (as you would a bamboo mat when making sushi) roll the filo over and tuck it under the cabbage filling. Continue rolling until you have a log-shaped pie.

Place it on a baking tray, seal-side down, and brush very generously all over with butter. Bake for 45 minutes on the middle shelf of the oven until crispy and golden brown. Serve with a side of garlicky dill yoghurt.

Lazanki

Cabbage and pasta might not be the most obvious combination at first glance, but take a closer look and the two ingredients seem almost inseparable in cuisines across the world. Chinese cabbage stir-fry with egg noodles, Italian *pizzoccheri*, German and Austrian *krautnideln* or *krautfleckerl*, the list goes on. Eastern European cuisine is rich in its own variations on the two ingredients, an influence from Germany, most likely. As with other dishes in this book these recipes are more of a culinary category, rather than a clear-cut set of cooking instructions. The two musts are the cabbage and the pasta, while the variations include bacon, mushrooms, sour cream, breadcrumbs and, of course, when it comes to pasta itself, the shapes are almost endless. This diversity is reflected in the name of the dish too: *lokshyna z kapustoiu* in Ukraine, *nudle s zelí* in the Czech Republic, Slovak *haluski* bear the same name in Romania and Poland, but this dish is also called *lazanki* in some regions of Poland as well as in neighbouring Belarus. In Hungary, there are three names for this dish: *káposztás tesztá*, *balushka* or *haluski*. While I struggled in most cases to see the correlation between the name of the dish and the shape of pasta used in it, *lazanki* is indeed the name of a pasta shape: bite-sized squares or rectangles. Here I offer you a cheat's version where instead of making your own *lazanki* from scratch you can use lasagne sheets broken into bite-sized bits (indeed some say that's what their name means anyway), or mix things up even more by using farfalle. The key is to cut your cabbage chunks into a similar size to the chosen pasta.

You can serve this simply with some finely chopped herbs. I also offer ideas for different toppings, including a pancetta and rye topping. With all these endless variations at your fingertips, this dish is a gift that keeps on giving.

Serves
4

- vegetable oil, for frying
- 1 onion, finely diced
- ½ small cabbage (about 400g/14oz)
- 1 teaspoon sugar
- 50g (1¾oz) salted butter
- 250g (9oz) pasta of choice
- salt and black pepper to taste

Heat some oil in a large lidded frying pan or a casserole (Dutch oven). Fry the onion (and pancetta, if using) on medium heat with a pinch of salt for 6–8 minutes, or until soft and translucent. Add the cabbage (and mushrooms, if using), season with salt, cover with the lid and cook for 15 minutes, until soft. Add a splash of water if it starts catching.

Add the sugar, take off the lid and cook for 10 minutes, or until the onion and the cabbage are caramelised.

In the meantime, bring a large saucepan of salted water to the boil and cook the pasta according to packet instructions. Once ready, tip into the casserole with the cabbage. Take off the heat, add the butter, and give it a good stir. Season with salt and pepper to taste (I like mine quite peppery).

PANCETTA AND RYE TOPPING

20g (¾oz) pancetta

vegetable oil, for frying

1–2 garlic cloves, finely grated

30g (1oz) rye bread, finely chopped

1 tablespoon honey

pinch of flaky sea salt

Fry the pancetta in a little oil for about 10–15 minutes, or until all the fat has melted and it's beginning to caramelise. Next, stir in the rye bread and honey, and fry for another 5–8 minutes, until the bread soaks up the fat and starts to crisp up. Add the garlic, stir through and take off the heat. Let it cool down enough to handle, transfer onto a chopping board, and give it a thorough chop with a knife, adding a pinch of sea salt at the end. Your topping is ready to be generously sprinkled on top of the finished pasta dish.

OTHER TOPPING IDEAS

sour cream

feta cheese or blue cheese

smoked paprika

fresh dill or parsley

30g (¾oz) smoked pancetta, fried

200g (7oz) fried mushrooms, cut in the same size chunks as your choice of pasta and the cabbage (see recipe introduction)

An Eastern European 'Spag Bol'

This whimsically titled recipe is inspired by my four-year-old daughter, Rosie. Like many kids her age she is a big fan of the good old spaghetti Bolognese, but unlike many kids (that I know of) she is an equally huge fan of sauerkraut. When she was a toddler, she used to refer to my homemade fermented cabbage as 'cabbagey noodles'. And rightly so, the long thin strips of cabbage are indeed very similar in shape to noodles. This gave me an idea to try a recipe where long cabbage stips would play the part of Italian pasta, and what could make for a better pairing with those than a Hungarian style sauce, richly flavoured with caraway, fennel seeds, dill and paprika. Rosie approved! And I hope so would you.

Serves
4–6

vegetable oil, for frying

1 onion, peeled and finely diced

1 carrot, peeled and grated

1 teaspoon dried dill

1 tablespoon Eastern European spice mix (½ teaspoon of each: coriander seeds, caraway seeds, fennel seeds lightly toasted and coarsely pounded)

1 tablespoon smoked paprika

½ teaspoon chilli powder (optional)

400g (14oz) minced (ground) beef or 200g (7oz) cooked green lentils and 200g (7oz) grated raw mushrooms

2 garlic cloves, finely chopped

2 x 400g (14oz) tins chopped tomatoes

1 teaspoon soft brown sugar

1 small cabbage (weighing approx. 450g/1lb)

1 small bunch of fresh dill, finely chopped

salt and black pepper, to taste

Heat the oil in a large casserole or ovenproof lidded frying pan and fry the onion and carrot with the dried dill, all the spices and a generous pinch of salt for 10 minutes over a medium heat.

Mix in the beef, season with salt, and cover with the lid. Cook for 5 minutes for the veggie version and 10 minutes for the meat version, stirring occasionally.

Add the garlic, mix well for a minute or so, then add the tomatoes, sugar and a pinch of salt. Cover with the lid and simmer for 8–10 minutes while you prepare the cabbage.

Using a knife or a mandoline, cut the cabbage into long strips resembling Italian tagliatelle.

Add the cabbage on top of the sauce, so that it retains its colour, season with salt, cover with the lid and cook until the cabbage is soft but still retains bite. At the end of the cooking, stir the cabbage through the sauce, generously sprinkle with the dill and serve with an optional dollop of sour cream or crème fraîche.

Bigos

Bigos is synonymous with Polish cuisine. However, a dish of stewed cabbage and sauerkraut richly flavoured with spices is common across Eastern Europe. I am still dreaming of the sauerkraut and roast pork dish I enjoyed with a pint of dark beer in Prague some 20 years ago! However, the Poles have perfected the practice of stewing sauerkraut into an artform! Despite its alternative names, 'the hunters' stew' and the more grotesque 'rascal's *bigos*', the dish is full of complex flavours worthy of haute cuisine. While it is hard to pinpoint the exact origin of the stew, it likely originated in the Polish-Lithuanian Commonwealth, and today is equally popular in Lithuania, Belarus and Ukraine. There are limitless variations on the types of meats and spices one can include, as long as there is cabbage, sauerkraut, wild mushrooms and prunes, you are guaranteed a truly memorable meal. Another rule is to always make *bigos* in a big batch – not only will it last you a few days, but its flavour will also get better along the way. Here, as with many recipes in the book, I offer a 'flexitarian' version.

Serves
6–8

- 60g (2oz) dried wild mushrooms
- vegetable oil, for frying
- 200g (7oz) Polish sausage or a mix of smoked pancetta and sausage (optional)
- 200g (7oz) stewing beef, diced (optional)
- 2 onions, peeled and thinly sliced
- 600g (1lb 5oz) shredded cabbage
- 600g (1lb 5oz) chestnut mushrooms (or 300g/10½oz if making a meat version)
- 600g (1lb 5oz) Classic Sauerkraut (see page 184) or shop-bought
- 2 bay leaves
- 4 allspice berries
- 1 scant tablespoon fennel seeds, lightly toasted and crushed
- 1 scant tablespoon caraway seeds, lightly toasted and crushed
- 120g (4¼oz) soft pitted prunes
- 400ml (14fl oz) meat or vegetable stock

Start by soaking the wild mushrooms in 100ml (3fl oz) just-boiled water. Set aside.

Heat a little oil in large heavy-based pan or a casserole (Dutch oven). If using meat, fry the sausage and beef over a medium heat for 10–12 minutes. Skip this step for the veggie version.

Add the onions with a pinch of salt and fry for 10–12 minutes, or until soft and translucent. Add the cabbage, fresh mushrooms and sauerkraut, together with all the spices, and let them cook while you deal with the wild mushrooms and prunes.

Strain the mushrooms through a fine sieve into a bowl, catching all the grit. Save the soaking liquid. Chop the mushrooms and prunes roughly, then add to the pan and give everything a good stir. Pour in the soaking liquid and half the stock, and let the stew do its own magic for 1 hour 30 minutes. Check on it every now and again and add more stock as it cooks away.

Leave it to cool down completely before refrigerating.

Reheat before serving and enjoy with boiled potatoes on the side.

CABBAGE ROLLS

Rather than seeing this as a single recipe, I envisage cabbage rolls as a culinary genre in their own right. This seemingly simple dish holds the key to a fascinating story of Eastern Europe, celebrating both its shared history and its regional diversity. A variation of cabbage leaves stuffed with a filling and poached in a sauce exists in every country of Eastern Europe (and the world), yet the exact recipes are as diverse as the names this dish carries.

Gołąbki in Poland, *halupki* in Czechia and Slovakia, *holubtsi* in Ukraine, *halubtsy* in Belarus, *holishkes* in the Ashkenazi communities, *szárma* in Hungary, *sarmale* in Moldova and Romania, *sarma* in the Roma communities, and *sarmi* in Bulgaria.

The etymology of these names is clear: on the one hand, there is the Turkish *sarması* from *sarmak*, which means 'roll' or 'packet' and, on the other, the Slavic root *holub* or *golab*, which means 'dove' or 'pigeon'. Perhaps not as obvious as the Turkish equivalent, the name is said to have been inspired by the rolls' shape and the way they nestle together in the baking dish as they cook.

Many food writers explain that the tradition of rolling flavourful fillings into cabbage leaves is likely to have come to the south of Eastern Europe via the Byzantine and the Ottoman Empires. Whereas in Turkey and Greece vine leaves are used to make *dolmas* or *dolmades* respectively, in Eastern Europe it is the glorious cabbage that takes their place (though the countries closest to Turkey and Greece use both).

Much plumper than their Mediterranean ancestors, the Eastern European rolls are eaten as a main course. Some recipes call for fresh leaves while others use fermented ones. When it comes to the stuffing and the poaching sauce there are many variations too: meat (pork and/or beef) and vegetarian (mainly mushroom), with rice or other popular grains like millet, buckwheat or pearl barley, poached or baked in a tomato or mushroom sauce flavoured with smoked paprika, caraway, coriander or sauerkraut brine, and/or soured cream, and topped with fresh dill or parsley. As Joan Nathan rightly notes, 'there are probably as many different stuffed cabbage recipes as there are towns in Central and Eastern Europe'. In fact, there is even an entire festival in the Transylvanian town of Praid, dedicated to stuffed cabbage rolls. Look it up! It's marvellous! (www.kaposztafesztival.eu)

Here I offer an amalgamation of several recipes: fermented cabbage leaves stuffed with meat and rice, and fresh cabbage leaves with a mushroom and pearl barley filling. I'd love to think that this section of the book will spark the *holishkes/sarmale* spirit in you, and you will feel free to experiment with your own flavours.

Cabbage Rolls with Sauerkraut Leaves, Beef and Rice in a Tomato Sauce

Serves
6–8

FOR THE ROLLS

100g (3½oz/½ cup) long grain white rice

vegetable oil, for frying

1 onion, peeled and finely diced

1 carrot, peeled and grated

4–6 garlic cloves, finely chopped

400g (14oz) minced (ground) beef

1 small bunch of dill, finely chopped

1 tablespoon ground coriander

1 teaspoon smoked paprika

10–12 Fermented Cabbage Leaves (see page 195) or fresh cabbage leaves

4 bay leaves

salt and black pepper, to taste

FOR THE SAUCE

2 x 400g (14oz) tins of finely chopped tomatoes

1 heaped teaspoon brown sugar

250ml (8½fl oz/1 cup) beef stock

Parboil the rice (check the packet instructions and halve the time) in very salty water, then drain and set aside.

Heat some vegetable oil in a large frying pan or casserole (Dutch oven) and fry the onion and carrot over a medium heat with a generous pinch of salt for 10–12 minutes, until golden and soft. Add the garlic, stir through and take off the heat.

Empty the contents into a large mixing bowl, add the beef, rice, dill, coriander and paprika, then give everything a thorough mix.

Preheat the oven to 200°C (400°F).

To make the rolls, place a cabbage leaf on a chopping board and add a heaped tablespoon of the filling onto the lower end of the leaf. Roll up the leaf as you would a burrito, tucking in the edges as you go along. Place seam-side down into the casserole used to fry the vegetables. Repeat with all the leaves and filling.

Nestle the rolls tightly into the dish, ideally into one layer, but you can make two, depending on the size and shape of your dish. Stick the bay leaves in between your rolls.

To make the sauce, season the tomatoes with the sugar, then add salt and pepper to taste. Mix with the stock and pour over the rolls.

Cover with a lid and bake for 2 hours, then remove the lid and bake for a further 10 minutes for the leaves to caramelise on top.

Serve with mashed potatoes or some bread.

Cabbage Rolls with Mushrooms and Pearl Barley in a Sour Cream Sauce

Serves
6–8

FOR THE ROLLS

sunflower or vegetable oil, for frying

100g (3½oz) pearl barley

1 onion, finely diced

1 carrot, peeled and grated

4–6 garlic cloves, finely chopped

400g (14oz) chestnut mushrooms

1 small cabbage

salt and black pepper to taste

FOR THE SAUCE

500ml (17fl oz/2 cups) mushroom stock, heated

300g (10½oz) sour cream

1 small bunch of parsley, chopped, to serve

Place the pearl barley into a medium saucepan of salted water, bring to a boil and cook for 30 minutes. Drain and set aside.

In a large casserole (Dutch oven), heat a drizzle of oil, and fry the onion and carrot over a medium heat with a pinch of salt for 10–12 minutes. Add the garlic and the mushrooms with another pinch of salt and cook for a further 8 minutes. Take off the heat, mix in the barley and let it cool down.

Meanwhile, bring a large pot of salt water to the boil for the cabbage.

Cut off the hard bottom stem from the cabbage, discard any damaged outer leaves and lower it into the water. Simmer for 5 minutes, until the first several layers come off easily but do not break. Carefully peel off as many as you can without effort. Repeat the process until you have 10–14 leaves. You can use the rest of the cabbage in soup, or stew.

Roll the cabbage with the filling following the instructions on page 48.

Preheat the oven to 200°C (400°F).

To make the sauce, mix the hot mushroom stock with the sour cream and season to taste.

Pour the sauce over the tightly nestled cabbage rolls, cover with a lid and bake for 10 minutes. Remove the lid and bake for another 10 minutes.

Sprinkle with the parsley before serving.

Varza A La Cluj – Romanian Sauerkraut, Meat and Grains Bake

There are endless possibilities for how you can use cabbage, meat and grains, and Eastern European cuisine presents us with just that. If I have cabbage, some type of grain and minced (ground) beef or mushrooms in my kitchen, I take comfort in the thought of just how many nourishing and delightful dishes I could make. *Varza a la Cluj* is a Romanian classic, not too dissimilar in flavour and ingredients to the cabbage rolls we've explored on the previous pages. However, this is a speedy, fuss-free version that requires no rolling and folding. The dish is believed to have originated in one of Transylvania's largest cities, Cluj, in the late 1600s, and it has been a widespread staple ever since. While this version is a meat one, have a look on page 52 for an alternative mushroom filling. I will also offer a choice of grains here, because who doesn't love an easy, nourishing and adaptable dish?

Serves
4–6

200g (7oz/1 cup) long grain white rice, or pearl barley or buckwheat

vegetable oil, for frying

2 onions, diced

2 carrots, peeled and grated

400g (14oz) minced (ground) beef

1 teaspoon dried dill

1 tablespoon smoked paprika

4 garlic cloves, finely chopped

500g (2 cups) passata (sieved tomatoes)

1 teaspoon sugar

4 bay leaves

600g (1lb 5oz) Classic Sauerkraut (see page 184) or shop-bought

250g (9oz) sour cream

smoked paprika, to sprinkle (optional)

sea salt, to taste

Parboil the grain of your choice (check the packet instructions and halve the cooking time), then drain and set aside.

In a large pan or casserole (Dutch oven), fry the onion and carrots over a medium heat in a little oil with a pinch of salt for 10 minutes, stirring occasionally. Add the beef mince and stir well until it starts to brown, about 8 minutes, then add the dill, paprika and garlic, and cook for a further 8–10 minutes.

Add the passata, sugar, bay leaves and salt to taste, and simmer over a low heat for 8–10 minutes.

Preheat the oven to 180°C (350°F).

Choose a deep, rectangular oven-proof baking dish and grease it with a bit of vegetable oil.

Place a third of the sauerkraut in the dish, top with half of the cooked grains, then add half the beef mixture. Repeat with another layer of sauerkraut, grains and beef, then finish with a final layer of sauerkraut.

Spread the sour cream evenly over the top, then add a sprinkle of smoked paprika for colour. Bake in the oven for 45 minutes.

It keeps really well in the fridge for 2–3 days.

Romani Cabbage and Chestnut Pie

I have to admit, I knew nothing about Romani cuisine before starting this book. Luckily, I have come across many fascinating sources, detailing the culinary customs of the Roma community. Similarly to the Ashkenazi Jews, the Roma adapted local cuisines to their religious and cultural beliefs, to the periods of hardships and scarcity, of which there were plenty, as well as to their nomadic lifestyle. As prolific foragers, they made the most of the edible ingredients available for free in nature, filling their cuisine with nuts, mushrooms and berries, which were often used to replace more expensive and unattainable foodstuffs, like meat. Humble vegetables, of course, are at the heart of Romani cuisine, and this recipe, which I have adapted from an old cookbook, is a delightful example of this tradition.

Serves
4–6

1 cabbage (800g–1kg/1lb 12oz–2lb 4oz)

2 tablespoons vegetable oil, plus extra for greasing

2 onions, diced

300g (10½oz) chestnut mushrooms, roughly chopped

4 garlic cloves, finely chopped

1 teaspoon finely chopped fresh thyme leaves, or dried thyme

150g (5½oz) cooked chestnuts, roughly chopped

100g (3½oz) Eastern European buckwheat, cooked according to packet instructions

50g (1¾oz) butter

salt and pepper to taste

sour cream, to serve

FOR THE TOPPING

150g (5½oz/1½ cups) dried breadcrumbs

1 teaspoon dried oregano or marjoram

1 teaspoon dried garlic powder

½ teaspoon cracked black pepper, plus more to taste

Bring a large saucepan of salted water to boil. Cut off the hard bottom stem from the cabbage, discard any damaged outer leaves, and lower it into the water. Simmer for 5 minutes, until the first several layers come off easily but do not break. Carefully peel as many as you can without effort, and repeat the process until you have 10–14 leaves, then set aside.

Heat the oil in a large frying pan or casserole (Dutch oven) and fry the onions over a medium heat with a pinch of salt for 10 minutes, until soft and translucent. Next, add the mushrooms, the garlic, thyme and the chestnuts with a pinch of salt. Cook for 10–12 minutes, stirring occasionally, until the mushrooms release their liquid. Stir in the cooked buckwheat and the butter, then stir well. Take off the heat, and let the flavours mingle.

Preheat the oven to 180°C (350°F). Grease a non-stick baking dish or loaf tin (roughly 28 x 16cm/11 x 6¼in) with oil.

Form the base of the pie from the softened cabbage leaves, lining the bottom and the sides tightly and making sure the leaves flap over the rim. Reserve 3–4 leaves.

Spoon in the mushroom and buckwheat mixture, and press tightly into the dish. Place the reserved leaves on top and flip the hanging ends back into the middle to seal the pie. Bake in the oven for 40 minutes.

While the pie is baking, prepare the topping by mixing the breadcrumbs, herbs, garlic and salt and pepper in a bowl.

When the pie is ready, flip it over onto an ovenproof tray (pan) or platter (some juices might splash out, so be careful!), sprinkle generously all over with the crumbs and return to the oven for 8–10 minutes for the crumbs to crisp up. Serve hot with a side of sour cream.

Cabbage and Fennel Braised in a Creamy Sauce

This recipe is inspired by a traditional Hungarian dish – *főzelék*. The premise could not be simpler: braise some shredded cabbage with onion in stock, then stir in the sour cream and dill and poach it a little longer. What a delight! However, I wanted to elevate this dish from a side to a main. The solution came from the popular global food trend to make steaks out of cabbage (and any brassicas). While I was in improvisation mode, I decided to throw in some fennel, as the two vegetables taste so good together. And here you have my cabbage and fennel 'steaks' braised in a creamy sauce, with tons of dill, naturally.

Serves
4

1 small cabbage (roughly 800g/1lb 12oz)

1 large fennel or 2 small ones

vegetable oil, for frying

a pinch of caster (superfine) sugar

1 onion, finely sliced

1 teaspoon fennel seeds, toasted and crushed

300ml (10fl oz) vegetable stock

2 bay leaves

250g (9oz) sour cream

2 tablespoons Dijon mustard

1 bunch of dill, finely chopped

salt and pepper, to taste

Cut the cabbage and the fennel into wedges, you should get 8 wedges of cabbage and 4–6 of the fennel.

Heat up some vegetable oil in a casserole (Dutch oven) or heavy-based lidded frying pan. Season the cabbage and fennel with salt and the sugar, and sear over a medium high heat on both sides for 10–12 minutes in total. Remove from the casserole and set aside.

Add another drizzle of oil, and fry the onion with some salt and fennel seeds for 8–10 minutes. Return the wedges to the casserole, pour in the stock and add the bay leaves, then simmer gently for 10 minutes.

Preheat the oven to 180°C (350°F).

Mix the sour cream with the mustard, and a few tablespoons of stock from the casserole to loosen the sauce up a little.

Pour into the casserole, then cook in the oven, without the lid, for 15 minutes, or until a golden crust is formed.

Sprinkle generously with the dill and serve from the casserole to show off the beauty of the dish.

BEETROOT

CHAPTER TWO

BEETROOT

Beetroot is the taste of home. My spirit vegetable. Dark in colour and sweet-earthy in flavour, her meaty texture is the flesh and her juice is the blood of Mother Earth herself. That dark, burgundy red turns a most delightful tender pink when mixed with sour cream – this unique shade of beetroot-sour-cream pink is the colour of my childhood memories. Would I have been a different person if I had never had the beetroot patties, bought and consumed on the way home from school, if I had never licked the ornate Bohemian-crystal bowl of beetroot, prune and walnut salad after each major family celebration, and if I had not eaten borsch weekly, cooked for me by the three generations of women in my family.

While beetroot's culinary history goes all the way back to the Roman era, it didn't come to Eastern Europe until the 16th century. Most likely, Germany and Italy are to thank for the introduction of this wonderful root vegetable to Eastern Europe, which soon became synonymous with the cuisine of the region. As my brief overview of my childhood beetroot-tinted memories shows, the uses of the vegetable are numerous. From salads to stews and soups, it also makes wonderful dips and spreads, pickles and ferments, and adds the most mysterious complexity to desserts.

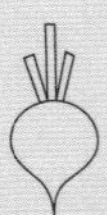

Beetroot Dips and Spreads

These recipes are exploding with all the wondrous beetroot flavours and demonstrate how an addition of just a few extra ingredients can create a whole new culinary experience out of this beautiful root vegetable. The dips and spreads can be enjoyed as part of a large Eastern European *zakąski* or *zakuski* feast, or as a stand-alone snack or breakfast in the form of a generously smothered chunky sourdough toast.

Serves
4

BEETROOT AND PLUM TWAROG

- 1 large raw beetroot (beet), peeled and grated, or cut into julienne
- 2 plums, slightly under-ripe
- 2 tablespoon cider apple vinegar
- 1 tablespoon honey
- 250g (9oz) Polish twarog (available from most Eastern European shops)
- zest of ½ lemon
- 1 small bunch of dill, roughly chopped
- salt and black pepper to taste
- 1 teaspoon poppy seeds, for sprinkling

Mix the beetroot in a bowl with the vinegar and honey.

Slice the plums into thin strips or matchsticks. Mix with the beetroot. Add the twarog, salt, pepper, lemon zest and dill.

Sprinkle with poppy seeds and serve with some rye bread.

SPICED BEETROOT WITH FRIED WALNUTS

- 3 tablespoons vegetable oil
- 1 onion, thinly sliced
- 500g (1lb 2oz) raw beetroots (beets), peeled and grated
- 2 garlic cloves, finely chopped
- 1 teaspoon balsamic vinegar
- 1 teaspoon mild clear honey
- a large pinch of chilli flakes
- sea salt flakes

FOR THE TOPPING

- a large handful of walnuts, roughly chopped
- 1 small bunch dill, stalks removed

Heat 1 tablespoon oil in a lidded frying pan over a medium heat. Add the onion with a pinch of salt and cook for 8–10 minutes, until softened. Add the grated beetroot and half the garlic, season with salt, add another tablespoon of oil and cook, stirring occasionally, for 10 minutes. Add a splash of water, cover with a lid, and simmer over a low heat for 20 minutes.

Meanwhile, make the topping. In a separate frying pan, heat the remaining oil over a low heat. Add the garlic and cook, infusing the oil, for 1 minute, stirring to prevent burning. Add the walnuts and cook for another minute, coating generously in the garlic oil. Remove from the heat and sprinkle with some sea salt flakes.

When the beetroot is cooked, add the vinegar, honey and chilli, and give it a good stir. Blend to a purée using a stick blender or in a food processor.

To serve, sprinkle with the garlicky walnuts and garnish with the dill.

BEETROOT, MAYO AND PRUNES

4 medium beetroots (beets), roasted (see page 62), or ready-cooked

12 soft juicy, pitted prunes, roughly chopped

50g (1¾oz) fresh walnuts, roughly chopped

2 garlic cloves, finely grated

4 heaped tablespooons mayonnaise (or crème fraîche or sour cream)

sea salt flakes, to taste

Put all the ingredients into a food processor and pulse several times until you get a chunky dip. (You can also use a hand blender.) Adjust the seasoning to your liking.

Originally this dish was served as a salad, so if you'd like to try that, then simply dice the beetroots, roughly chop the prunes and walnuts, and mix with garlic and mayonnaise, or sour cream.

BEETROOT AND EGG GARLICKY MAYO SPREAD

2 medium raw beetroots (beets), roasted (see page 62), or ready-cooked

2 hard-boiled eggs, peeled

1 garlic clove, finely grated

2 heaped tablespoons mayonnaise

1 teaspoon horseradish cream, or to taste

1 heaped tablespoon chopped parsley

flaky sea salt and ground black pepper to taste

Grate the beetroots and eggs into a medium bowl.

Add the garlic, the mayonnaise the horseradish cream and parsley. Give it a thorough mix with a fork. Taste and season with salt and pepper to your liking.

Taratuta – Ukrainian Beetroot, Gherkin and Horseradish Salad

This recipe has been generously shared with me by Olga Koutseridi, a Ukrainian historian, baker and food writer from Texas. Here is what she says about this dish:

'This dish has two forms: it comes as a cold summer soup and as a salad. I absolutely love the salad version, which is colourful and simple and traditionally has been served during Lent in eastern Ukraine as far back as the 15th century. The salad comes together swiftly with only five ingredients if you count the gherkins (dill pickles) and the brine as one. Make sure to look for unrefined sunflower oil for a real taste of Ukraine. If you are having a hard time finding fresh horseradish, you can use jarred horseradish instead.'

Serves
4–6

2 large beetroots (beets), boiled or roasted (see page 62), or ready-cooked, and diced

100g (3½oz) gherkins (dill pickles), diced

1 small red onion, finely diced

2 tablespoon grated horseradish

1 teaspoon gherkin (dill pickle) brine, or more to taste

2–3 tablespoons unrefined sunflower oil

sea salt, to taste

In a large mixing bowl, mix together the beetroots, gherkins and onion.

Now add the horseradish, brine and oil. You might need to adjust the brine amount to find the right balance of sourness, but this will depend on the pickles. Lightly season with salt.

Herby Smetana Bed with Colourful Beets

Inspired by a traditional Eastern European summer salad dressing of sour cream (smetana) with dill, this dish would fit beautifully on a late-summer table. The vividly herbaceous bed of green sour cream, capturing all the vibrant flavours of summer, hosts a bounty of roasted colourful beetroots, a hint of the cosy autumnal roasts to come. This works well as a side dish or a starter. The dish is rounded off with a drizzle of sunflower oil and a sprinkle of toasted seeds; their warm earthy flavour binds everything together with an Eastern European accent.

Serves
4–6

FOR THE ROASTED BEETROOTS

4 tablespoons sunflower oil

4 medium or large beetroots (beets) of different colours, peeled

1 small garlic bulb

sea salt flakes, to taste

FOR THE HERBY SMETANA BED

300g (1¼ cups) sour cream

1 small garlic clove, finely chopped

1 tablespoon lemon juice

1 small bunch of each: coriander (cilantro), dill, parsley, mint, finely chopped

1 tablespoon toasted sunflower seeds

unrefined cold-pressed sunflower oil

sea salt flakes and black pepper, to taste

Preheat the oven to 200°C (400°F).

I like to use two trays (tins) to roast the vegetables as the beetroot should crisp and caramelise rather than steam (when overcrowded, this tends to be the result).

Divide the oil equally between two roasting trays and heat it up in the oven.

Cut the beetroots into bite-sized wedges. Remove the roasting trays from the oven and add the beetroots and whole bulb of garlic to the sizzling oil. Using a spoon, coat the vegetables in the hot oil, then season with sea salt flakes. Roast for 40–45 minutes, or until caramelised and cooked through.

Meanwhile, prepare the herby smetana bed. In a large bowl, mix all the ingredients. Taste and adjust acidity and seasoning as you prefer. The dip will be thick with greens.

To serve, spread the smetana on a large platter (or you can use two smaller plates). Pop the roasted garlic out of its skins and place on top with the roasted beetroots. Drizzle with some sunflower oil and sprinkle with the sunflower seeds. Finish with a final seasoning of sea salt flakes.

BORSCH

On 7 July 2022 UNESCO has inscribed 'the culture of Ukrainian borsch cooking' onto its intangible cultural heritage list. This gesture may finally help lay to rest the old-age debate of 'where borsch comes from'. While the diversity of borsch recipes across Ukraine is indeed unparalleled by any other part of Eastern Europe, and hence the UNESCO status, variations of the soup also exist in other countries. In Poland it is known as *barszcz*, the North American Ashkenazi community spell it as borscht, and a Lithuanian version of a cold borsch, called *šaltibarščiai*, is popular all around the world.

While borsch is believed to have developed from a Slavic hogweed soup (giving it both its tang and its name) we can make a wild leap even further into the past and find a borsch prototype in ancient Rome. Marcus Terentius Varro (116–27 BC) a noted scholar of the Roman Empire, wrote extensively on agriculture, and included numerous (mostly medicinal) recipes in his works. There we find a recipe for beetroot stock (used for curing digestive ailments), and it's not too irrational to see that recipe as a precursor to the iconic Ukrainian soup.

However, we now face a major question: is beetroot (beet) an integral part of borsch? You might be surprised to hear the answer is 'no', or rather 'it depends on the region'. In Southern Ukraine, tomatoes are valued over beetroot, a green borsch (aka a sorrel soup) is also widely enjoyed across Eastern Europe, and Poland and the neighbouring parts of Belarus prepare a white *barszcz*, also known as *zurek*. In Romania they make a type of soup called *barš*, which, although sounds like its Ukrainian neighbour, is in fact a cousin of zurek and has very little to do with the original borsch itself, apart from their shared tangy quality.

As for other ingredients, things are even less clear cut. All types of meat are welcome, and fish is also used in the coastal areas of Ukraine, most famously the Odesan borsch with carp, which is said to have been the favourite of Taras Shevchenko, Ukrainian poet, painter and freedom fighter. A vast array of vegetables and pulses is commonly included, from red peppers to mushrooms and fresh or fermented cabbage. Even fruit like smoked prunes and pears can be found in some regional recipes. Many consider the marker of a good borsch to be a consistency so thick that a ladle or a spoon that can stand up in it unaided, however, there are also clear beetroot broths such as that used in the Western Ukrainian and Polish Christmas borsch with dumplings called (*vushka* or *uszka*), or the summer clear cold borsch with diced fresh vegetables and herbs.

The one thing that all borsch soups have in common is the complexity of their flavour – a delicate balance between sweet, earthy, salty, tangy and sharp. This is what makes borsch simply the best kind of soup in the world (in my humble opinion).

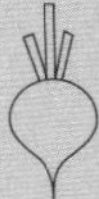

Classic Beef Borsch

Serves
6

FOR THE STOCK (BROTH)

500g (1lb 2oz) stewing beef chunks (you can add some beef bones if available)

2 bay leaves

1 teaspoon black peppercorns

1 teaspoon coriander seeds

1 teaspoon fennel seeds

1 tablespoon fine sea salt

handful of parsley or dill stalks

1 onion, skin-on, halved

1 carrot, scrubbed, skin on

2 celery sticks

FOR THE SOUP

vegetable oil, for frying

1 onion, diced

1 large carrot, peeled and grated

2 large or 4 medium beetroots (beets), peeled and grated

4 tablespoons tomato purée

scant 1 tablespoon soft brown sugar

1 red (bell) pepper, sliced into thin strips

½ medium white cabbage, sliced into thin strips

1 x 400g (14oz) tin red kidney beans, drained and rinsed

2 garlic cloves, finely crushed

1 tablespoon apple cider vinegar or sauerkraut brine

1 large bunch of dill, chopped

sea salt and black pepper, to taste

TO SERVE (PER PLATE)

1 tablespoon sour cream

1 tablespoon chopped dill

1 slice of toasted rye bread

1 garlic clove, cut in half

To make the stock, place all the ingredients into a large saucepan and cover with 3 litres (101fl oz/12 cups) water. Bring to the boil, lower the heat and simmer for 2 hours, occasionally removing the froth from the top with a slotted spoon. Top up with water as needed, and adjust the salt level as you wish. When the stock is ready, strain through a sieve into a bowl, discarding all the vegetables, bay leaves and spices. You can give the meat chunks a quick rinse to wash off some froth and the spices. Some coriander and fennel seeds will make their way into the soup, which is a very welcome addition.

Next make the soup. Heat the oil in a large frying pan and fry the onion, carrots and beetroot with a pinch of salt over a medium heat for 15–20 minutes, until soft. If it starts to catch, add a ladle of the stock from the pan.

Next, add the tomato purée and sugar, mix well and cook for another 8–10 minutes.

Put the saucepan in which you made the stock back over a medium heat and tip in the contents of the frying pan. Then pour in the stock, add the cabbage, pepper strips, kidney beans, crushed garlic and vinegar. Allow to simmer for 15–20 minutes. Towards the end of the cooking time, add the dill and taste for seasoning. Turn off the heat and leave the soup to rest, covered, for 40 minutes.

Serve in individual bowls topped with sour cream, dill and black pepper. A piece of toasted rye bread (generously rubbed with a cut garlic clove) on the side is a must.

Vegan Borsch with Mushrooms and Prunes

Serves
6

30g (1oz) dried wild mushrooms

vegetable oil, for frying

1 onion, peeled and diced

1 carrot, peeled and grated

2 small–medium beetroots (beets), peeled and grated

2 litres (68fl oz/8 cups) vegetable stock

1 teaspoon dried dill

1 tablespoon allspice berries

2 bay leaves

2 large potatoes, peeled and cubed

⅓ medium white cabbage (200–300g/7–10½oz), shredded

1 x 400g (14oz) tin red kidney beans, drained and rinsed

2 garlic cloves, finely grated

70g (2½oz) pitted prunes, roughly chopped

100g (3½oz) Classic Sauerkraut with plenty of brine (see page 184), or shop-bought

1 handful of dill, chopped

sour cream, to serve (optional)

Soak the wild mushrooms in 500ml (17fl oz/2 cups) hot water and set aside while you prepare the rest of the borsch.

Heat the oil in a large saucepan and fry the onion over a medium heat for 8 minutes, until softened. Add the carrot and beetroots with a pinch of salt and sauté for 10 minutes.

Strain the mushrooms, getting rid of the grit, and reserve the soaking liquid. Roughly chop and add to the pan along with the stock, the dill, a generous pinch of salt, the mushroom soaking liquid, and the allspice and bay leaves.

Bring to the boil, add the potatoes, shredded cabbage, kidney beans, garlic, and prunes. Simmer for 45 minutes then add the sauerkraut.

Take off the heat, let cool down completely and leave the borsch in the fridge overnight (oh the patience this step requires!).

To serve, heat in the same pan, remove the allspice berries, ladle into bowls, then add some dill and a dollop of sour cream (if opting out of a vegan version).

Kapusta

Chłodnik – Cold Borsch with Kefir

Serves
4

3 large beetroots (beets), peeled and cut in half

3 garlic cloves, crushed

1 onion, peeled and halved

1 carrot, scrubbed and cut into chunks

4 allspice berries

1 tablespoon salt

1 tablespoon apple cider vinegar or 4 tablespoons sauerkraut brine (choose any from Chapter 7, or use shop-bought)

FOR THE TOPPING

50–100ml (1¾fl oz–3½fl oz) kefir (per plate)

1 cucumber, peeled and diced

4 radishes, diced

8 tablespoons mixed fresh herbs (dill, parsley, chives)

Place all the ingredients except the vinegar (or sauerkraut brine) into a large saucepan with 1.5 litres (51fl oz/6 cups) water and salt well. Bring to the boil, then lower the heat and simmer over a medium heat for 40 minutes to 1 hour. Take off the heat and let it cool and infuse at room temperature. Once cooled, transfer to a fridge for a few hours.

Strain the soup through a fine sieve – you might want to line the sieve with a muslin (cheesecloth) to catch any fine particles. Discard all the vegetables apart from the beetroots and set aside.

Add the vinegar or sauerkraut brine and adjust to taste. It needs to be sweet, earthy and tangy. Finely dice the cooked beetroot.

Ladle into four bowls. Swirl the kefir through, then top with the diced vegetables and herbs.

You might want to keep some horseradish cream on standby!

Beetroot and Kidney Bean Stew with Chard and Feta

Admittedly, this dish is not a classic of Eastern European cuisine, and I am pushing the territorial borders a little here, moving closer to the Caucasus or the Balkans, but I simply could not exclude a recipe so dear to my heart. I have a handful of recipes that have travelled with me through life, being my source of comfort at various stages. In this case, moving into my first flat as a PhD student, I conjured up this dish to impress my boyfriend (now life partner) during the early stages of our romance, later nourishing myself with it after giving birth to both our children, and then introducing (a simplified version) to our babies as one of their first foods (to great success I might add). Featuring the queen of my kitchen – the beetroot – this dish also marries other undeniably perfect ingredients together – red kidney beans, walnuts, earthy coriander and smoky paprika with tangy and creamy feta. If Eastern European cuisine is part of your culinary DNA, I am sure this dish will taste like home. And, if not, this is simply a super-easy, nourishing and flavourful meal to add to your kitchen repertoire.

Serves
4–6

vegetable oil, for frying

2 onions, cut into half-moons

2 pinches of salt

2 garlic cloves, finely chopped or grated

2 teaspoons ground coriander

1 teaspoon smoked paprika

½ teaspoon chilli powder (optional)

4–5 medium beetroots (beets), peeled and cut into thin wedges

1 tablespoon pomegranate molasses

1 x 400g (14oz) tin of red kidney beans, drained and rinsed

200g (10½oz) chard (or beetroot tops or spinach)

50g (1¾oz) walnuts, roughly chopped

50g (1¾oz) feta, crumbled

a handful of dill

crusty bread, to serve

Heat a little oil in a casserole (Dutch oven) or large saucepan with a lid.

Add the onions with the salt, and cook over amedium heat for 10–12 minutes. Then add the garlic and the spices and fry for a further 5 minutes, stirring occasionally. Add the beetroots and the pomegranate molasses. Pour in enough water to just cover the beetroots, and cook over medium heat for 30 minutes or until soft but still with bite.

Add the beans and the greens, stir well and cook for 2–3 minutes. Sprinkle with the walnuts, feta and dill before serving with a chunky slice of bread to mop up the gorgeous beetroot-feta sauce.

Kapusta

Rye, Beetroot and Beef Meatballs with Coriander and Gherkins

Eastern European meatballs, like many dishes in this book, are a genre, rather than a dish, born out of the fascinating history of the region. On the one hand, there is the influence of the Greek and Turkic *koftas*, on the other there are the cutlettes and the croquettes of Western European cuisine, which at various points exerted a huge influence on the various Eastern European empires. The Soviet and the Socialist eras saw a huge explosion in popularity of meatballs, aka meat patties, which became a genuine staple in the 'workers' canteens' and in homes (where the bread to meat ratio was in your favour).

This recipe is an improvisation on all the best flavours that I have gleaned from recipes across the regions of Eastern Europe. If you have never tried grating a pickled gherkin into your meatball mixture, I suggest you drop this book immediately and go to the kitchen. Well, do read the recipe first, of course.

Makes
20

- 400g (14oz) beef mince
- 2 raw beetroots (beets) (weighing approx. 250g/9oz), peeled and grated
- 4 garlic cloves, finely chopped
- 2 gherkins (dill pickles), grated
- 2 eggs
- 1 large slice of rye bread (60g/2oz), soaked in beef stock for 1 minute, then squeezed
- 4 heaped tablespoons chopped dill
- 2 tablespoons ground coriander
- generous pinch of salt and black pepper
- vegetable oil, for shallow-frying
- slaw and mustard or horseradish sauce, or Tovchanka (page 92), to serve

In a large bowl, thoroughly mix all the ingredients together with your hands.

Shape the mixture into small, slightly flattened balls, around 50g (1¾oz). (You may prefer to make them bigger, and use them as burger patties.)

To fry the meatballs, heat enough oil (4–6 tablespoons) for shallow-frying over medium heat (the exact amount of oil will depend on the size of the pan). Fry in batches over medium heat for 10 minutes, turning occasionally so they are browned on all sides.

Serve with a slaw on the side and some mustard or horseradish sauce for dipping. Or you can (and should) up your 'meatballs and mash' game to the next level by serving these with Tovchanka.

Beetroot and Rye Chocolate Cake

Beetroot's natural sweetness and earthiness makes it a perfect ingredient in cakes, especially those containing chocolate and rye flour. Although this is not a traditional recipe of a specific Eastern European country or region, I felt it held true to the essence of Eastern European baking. It was a pleasure to ask one of my favourite bakers, Polina Chesnakova, to develop this recipe for the book. Polina, like myself, and other contributors to this book, comes from a mixed Eastern European heritage, and now lives in the United States.

Makes 1 x 20cm (8in) cake (8–10 SLICES)

80g (2¾oz) plain (all-purpose) flour

50g (1¾oz) rye flour

40g (1½oz) natural cocoa powder

¾ teaspoons baking soda

¾ teaspoon fine sea salt

½ teaspoon instant espresso powder (optional)

100g (3½oz) sugar

100g (3½oz) light brown sugar

2 large eggs, room temperature

190g (6½oz) puréed beetroot (beet) (from about 2 medium beetroots, cooked and finely grated or pulsed in a food processor, with excess liquid removed)

115g (4oz) neutral oil, such as rapeseed (canola)

1 teaspoon vanilla extract

cocoa (unsweetened chocolate) powder or icing (powdered) sugar, (optional), for dusting

FOR THE CHOCOLATE GANACHE (OPTIONAL)

85g (3oz) dark chocolate, finely chopped

85ml (3fl oz) double (heavy) cream

2 teaspoons clear honey

1½ teaspoons kirsch, orange liqueur, or other liqueur (optional)

pinch of fine sea salt

Preheat the oven to 180°C (350°F) and grease and line a 20cm (8in) springform round cake tin (pan).

Sift the flours, cocoa powder, baking soda, salt, and, if using, espresso powder into a large bowl. Add both sugars and whisk together to evenly distribute. Use your fingers to break up any clumps.

In a bowl, whisk together the eggs, beetroot purée, oil, and vanilla until smooth. Fold the wet mixture into the flour mixture, until fully incorporated and a smooth batter has formed.

Scrape the batter into the prepared tin. Bake for about 30 minutes, or until a tester inserted in the centre of the cake comes out clean. Transfer to a wire rack and allow the cake to cool completely before transferring to a plate. If not making ganache, dust with cocoa powder or icing sugar.

To make the chocolate ganache, put the chocolate into a small bowl. In a small saucepan, bring the cream and honey to a simmer over a medium-low heat. Pour the mixture over the chocolate and let sit, undisturbed, for 1 minute. Gently stir until smooth. Stir in the liqueur and salt. You can make this in advance as it will keep for up to 1 week in the fridge, just gently warm through before using.

Slowly pour the ganache evenly over the top of the cake, allowing it to drip down the sides. If you would like, let it set for 30 minutes to an hour before serving. The cake keeps well wrapped at room temperature for 3–4 days.

POTATO

CHAPTER THREE

POTATO

Although potatoes did not arrive on the European continent until the 16th century, and perhaps even more surprisingly until the 19th century to Eastern Europe, they have rapidly become a staple food for the rich and the poor, as well as within marginalised communities like the Ashkenazi Jews and the Roma. In Belarus, for example, they have become known as the 'second bread'. Providing the necessary sustenance in absence of protein as a main ingredient, these starchy wonders work equally well as a side dish. In fact, I would struggle to think of a better vegetable to accompany your memorable feasts as well as your simple weekday dinners. Potatoes have had a fair share of bad PR, being labelled as boring and bland. However, in Eastern European cuisine they are a real pillar; a foundation that holds up the entire culinary culture and the stuff many formative memories are made of. And they are absolutely delicious, may I add!

To me the indisputable winner is my gran's mashed potato – light, fluffy, creamy and sweet, whipped by hand with abundant amounts of full-fat milk, butter and a final touch of egg yolk. An equally heart-warming memory would be of a moment when I'd mash cubes of potato cooked in a rich chicken broth with the back of a spoon to build the perfect spoonful of potato, chicken meat and broth. Cold potatoes deserve praise of their own, too. Starting with simple cold mash, which I could eat straight out of the fridge with a slice of rye bread, to simple salads of boiled potatoes dressed with lashings of unrefined sunflower oil, a mountain of dill and thinly sliced red onion; not to mention the delicious mayo-dressed salads of boiled potatoes and gherkins. In this chapter, we will explore the whole spectrum of dishes that the humble potato can yield.

POTATO SALADS

This section could easily be turned into a chapter of its own, so diverse and delicious is the repertoire of potato salads in the cuisine of the region. The tradition of using potatoes in salads is believed to have originated in Germany in the 16th century, from where it then migrated East. Polish potato salads are arguably the best known Eastern European versions of the original German tradition, however, mayonnaise- or cream-dressed potatoes can be found all across Eastern Europe (and beyond). If we travel east to the furthest part of Europe we will find the Olivier salad aka the Russian salad, which was created at the end of the 19th century in Moscow, and peaked in popularity during the second half of the Soviet era (1950s onwards), spreading widely not only across Soviet-controlled Eastern European countries (Ukraine, Moldova and Belarus) but across the Eastern bloc more widely (Poland, Hungary, Romania, Czechoslovakia, Bulgaria). I begin this section with the most iconic recipe, the Polish potato and gherkin mayonnaise salad (a close relative of the Olivier), which is a real winter staple that speaks of comfort to me. I also offer lighter seasonal variations, making a nod to the Baltic and Nordic cuisines via the potato and fennel salad with dill and mustard dressing, and celebrate the flavours of the summer with a crunchy, herby new potato salad dressed in tangy sour cream. These dishes can be eaten alone, as a side to some grilled meat or fish, or as part of a larger summer picnic spread or a barbecue party where the crunchy new potato salad would be the perfect guest.

Polish Potato and Gherkin Salad

Serves
4

1 large carrot, peeled

3 potatoes of the same size, peeled

3 eggs

4 medium gherkins (dill pickles) or 2 large sour cucumbers

4 heaped tablespoons mayonnaise

2 heaped teaspoons Dijon mustard

25g (1oz) dill, finely chopped

2 pinches of flaky sea salt

black pepper to taste

4 rye bread slices to serve

Put the carrots and potatoes in a large saucepan, cover with cold salted water and boil until cooked through but not mushy. Remove from the pan and cook the eggs in the same water for 12 minutes.

While the eggs cook, chop the gherkins into equal-sized small cubes. This is a real test of your knife skills.

In a large bowl, mix together the mayonnaise, mustard and dill, and season with salt and pepper. Taste, and adjust the seasoning or the amount of mustard to your liking. Add the vegetables to the bowl.

When the eggs are ready, peel and dice them in a shape similar to the rest of the veggies. Mix everything well to evenly coat the vegetables and eggs in the dressing.

Chill in the fridge for a few hours before serving, if you have the patience. Make sure to have a slice of rye bread on the side.

Fennel and Potato Salad with Mustard and Dill

Serves
4

500g (1lb 2oz) new potatoes

1 large fennel

1 red onion

2 tablespoons apple cider vinegar

salt and black pepper to taste

FOR THE DRESSING

50ml (1¾fl oz) unrefined sunflower oil

1 tablespoon honey

1 tablespoon wholegrain mustard

1 tablespoon Dijon mustard

1 tablespoon apple cider vinegar, or to taste

25g (1oz) dill, roughly chopped

Cook the potatoes in salted water for 30 minutes, or until cooked through but firm. Drain the potatoes and let them cool down before cutting each in half lengthways.

Thinly slice the fennel and the red onion on a mandoline. Place in a bowl and toss with the vinegar and a pinch of salt.

Make the dressing by mixing the oil, honey, mustard and vinegar. Season the dressing to taste.

Add the potatoes to the bowl with the fennel and onions, throw in the dill, pour in the dressing and give everything a good mix.

СМЕТАНА
cream
0%

Summer Potato Salad

Serves
4

- 350g (12½oz) baby potatoes
- 6 radishes
- ½ large cucumber
- 3–4 ripe tomatoes
- 1 small red (bell) pepper
- 15g (½oz) dill, chopped
- 15g parsley, chopped
- 15g chives or spring onions (scallions), chopped
- 1 tablespoon unrefined sunflower oil
- 1 tablespoon apple cider vinegar
- 200g (7oz) sour cream
- salt and black pepper to taste
- 4 rye bread slices, to serve

Here you can either dice all the vegetables in to equal sizes or, to give the salad a more rustic feel, slice the radishes into rounds, dice the cucumber and the pepper, and quarter the potatoes and the tomatoes.

Cook the potatoes in a large saucepan of salted water for 20 minutes, or until easily pierced with a knife, but still firm. Drain.

Place the potatoes in a bowl with all the vegetables and the herbs, dress with oil, vinegar and sour cream. Generously season with salt and pepper, and serve immediately.

Make sure to have some rye bread on the table to mop up the pool of sour cream dressing that will be left at the bottom of the salad bowl.

Qistibi – Tatar Potato Flatbreads

This delightfully simple dish is a staple in the cuisines of the Volga Tatars as well as of the Chuvash people, a fellow Turkic ethnic group residing in the Eastern European part of Russia. These flatbreads would be the identical twins of the Turkish *gözleme* were it not for the filling. They are traditionally filled with rice or millet porridge, but mashed potatoes are sometimes used instead. This recipe was kindly given to me by Firuza Yusupova, a pastry chef of a Tatar-Jewish origin, whose family story spans the area between Bashkortostan and Samarkand, and is written through recipes and food memories passed down from one generation to the next, preserving and celebrating their Tatar heritage.

Makes
8 (LARGE QISTIBI)

FOR THE DOUGH

250ml (8½fl oz/1 cup) water

50g (1¾oz) butter, melted, plus extra for brushing

2 tablespoons sour cream

500g (1 lb 2oz) plain (all-purpose) flour

½ teaspoon salt

1 teaspoon caster (superfine) sugar

FOR THE FILLING

5–6 medium potatoes (weighing approx. 600g/1 lb 5oz), peeled and diced

vegetable oil, for frying

2 onions, peeled and thinly sliced

50g (1¾oz) salted butter

salt and pepper to taste

To make the dough, mix together all the ingredients in a large bowl. Work the dough until it comes together easily into a ball. Cover with cling film (plastic wrap) and let it rest for 30 minutes.

To make the filling, cook the potatoes in salted water for 10–15 minutes until soft.

In the meantime, heat a little oil in a frying pan and fry the onions with a pinch of salt over a medium heat for 15 minutes, until soft and caramelised in places.

When the potatoes are cooked, mash them roughly with the salted butter, add the onions and season with salt and pepper. (I like my filling quite peppery as this gives the potatoes a satisfying depth and warmth, but let your tastebuds guide you.)

Return to the dough, tip it out onto a dusted surface, knead it for a few minutes, divide it into balls (40g/1½oz each), then roll each into a thin disc about 20cm (8in) in diameter. Keep the rolled dough discs under a tea towel while you finish the rest.

Heat a non-stick frying pan and toast each flatbread on both sides until golden brown. Stack the cooked flatbreads under a dish towel. When all the flatbreads are ready, stuff them with 2–3 heaped tablespoons of the potato mash and fold in half. Generously brush with the melted butter and serve immediately.

You can easily reheat these by toasting the flatbread in a dry pan on each side for a few moments and drizzling some hot melted butter over the top to finish.

Tovchanka – Ukrainian Potato and Bean Mash

I was already a loyal fan of good old mash, but this dish expanded my understanding of just how delicious mashed potatoes can be, beyond all expectations. Originating in Western Ukraine (in the Galician Ternopil) *tovchanka* consists of buttery potatoes, mashed with beans and poppy seeds. Some variations include onions and sugar, too. Forgive me for changing the recipe method slightly, as I braise the potatoes and the beans together in a broth with caramelised onions and spices to bring out the maximum flavour potential of the dish. It really is one of the most delicious ways to cook potatoes and if you are like me, you'll probably wonder where this recipe has been all your life!

Serves
4

vegetable oil, for frying

1 large onion, peeled and thinly sliced

4 medium-large potatoes (weighing approx. 600g/1lb 5oz), peeled and diced

1 x 400g (14oz) tin cannellini beans, drained and rinsed

250–350ml (8½–12fl oz) vegetable or chicken stock

2 bay leaves

2–3 allspice berries

70g (2½oz) butter

salt and black pepper to taste

2–4 tablespoons salted butter

2–4 tablespoons poppy seeds

Heat the oil in a large deep casserole (Dutch oven) or large saucepan and fry the onion over a medium heat with a pinch of salt for 8 minutes, or until soft and translucent.

Add the potatoes and beans and pour in the stock (the stock should just cover the potatoes). Add the bay leaves and the allspice berries and cook for 10–15 minutes until the potatoes are tender.

Take off the heat, discard the berries and the bay leaves, add the butter, season to taste and blitz with a handblender or roughly mash using a potato masher.

Melt the butter in a small saucepan or frying pan and mix the poppy seeds through for 1 minute or so. Drizzle on top of the mash before serving.

Knishes – Ashkenazi Buns with Potato and Sour Cream

I usually don't play favourites with my food, but I am afraid I have to say that Slavic *piroshki* stand no chance against their Ashkenazi siblings – *knishes*. I have to confess, as someone who grew up eating *piroshki*, it never crossed my mind to make *knishes*. However, once I did, my heart was won over. Very quick and relatively easy to make, these little bundles boast the most perfect flaky buttery pastry and can be filled with anything from mince meat to mashed potatoes, sauerkraut, mushrooms and buckwheat; some recipes also offer sweet alternatives of twarog and jam. Consumed as a snack or a side to a soup, knishes are usually baked but can also be deep-fried.

Knishes hail from the Ashkenazi diaspora in Ukraine, Belarus and Poland, where they are known as *knysh* or *knysz* (the word's etymology goes back to German *knitschen* to 'crumple'), and they were popularised worldwide by the Ashkenazi immigrants to the USA in the early 20th century. New York is their hometown and if you happen to be there, make sure to pay a visit to the Yonah Schimmel Knish Bakery, steeped in over 100 years of Ashkenazi history, and the only surviving *knish* bakery in what used to be Manhattan's Knish Alley. Having fallen out of favour over the last several decades, the humble buns are said to be making a comeback, so there is no better time than now to join the fan club with me.

Makes
14

FOR THE FILLING

vegtable oil, for frying

50g (1¾oz) butter

2 onions, peeled and thinly sliced

1 teaspoon caster (superfine) sugar

4–5 potatoes, peeled and quartered

4 tablespoons sour cream

2 tablespoons chopped chives or dill

salt and black pepper to taste

FOR THE DOUGH

350g (12½oz), plain (all-purpose) flour, plus extra for dusting

1 teaspoon baking powder

½ teaspoon fine salt

½ teaspoon caster (superfine) sugar

Start by making the the filling. Heat a little oil in a frying pan, add 10g (¼oz) of butter and fry the onion with a pinch of salt and the sugar over a low heat, stirring occasionally, for 30 minutes or until soft and caramelised.

Place the potatoes in a large saucepan of cold salted water, bring to boil and simmer for 25 minutes, or until cooked but still firm.

To make the dough, mix together the dry ingredients in a large bowl.

In another bowl, mix the wet ingredients. Make a well in the dry ingredients and pour in the wet mixture. Start mixing with a spoon first, then use your hands to gradually incorporate the ingredients to form a dough. Once it comes together into a ball, tip on to a clean, dry dusted surface and knead for 2–3 minutes. Put back into the bowl, cover with clingfilm and let rest while you get back to the filling.

Drain the potatoes, add the remaining 40g (1½oz) butter, and mash roughly with a potato masher. Add the rest of the ingredients and give a thorough mix. Set aside to cool down, while you get back to the dough.

Preheat the oven to 180°C (350°F).

1 large egg, slightly beaten, plus 1 egg mixed with a splash of water for egg wash

120ml (4fl oz) warm water

120ml (4fl oz) vegetable oil

1 teaspoon white vinegar

Divide the dough into two halves. Put one back into the bowl and cover with clingfilm while you work with the other half. Dust the surface with some flour and roll the dough out into a large rectangle, as thin as you possibly can. Some traditional Jewish recipes recommend making it as thin as a table cloth. Trim off the wonky edges.

Take half the filling and shape it into a log across the longest side of the dough rectangle, roughly 1cm (½in) from the edge of the dough. Pull the dough over the filling and continue rolling until the log is lying in front of you, seam-side down.

Keep rolling it back and forth to make sure the filling is evenly distributed and the seam is not as pronounced. Pinch the ends and cut off any excess dough.

Now comes the fun part… If you have a good eye for proportion, divide the log into equal segments of roughly 6–7cm (2½–2¾in) long: make subtle incisions with the blunt end of the knife, but don't cut all the way through.

Next, use the side of your hand to cut through the incisions and seal each bun that way. Pick up each *knish*, seal the bottom and the top and squash it a little to give it that distinct *knish* shape.

Place on a baking sheet, leaving a bit of space in between, and make a little indentation in the middle of each *knish* with your thumb. Brush generously with egg wash and bake for 45 minutes, rotating halfway through.

Allow to cool a little before serving. These taste best warm or at room temperature.

Kartoplianyky – Ukrainian Potato Pasties

This dish is a delicious example of just how many wonderful meals you can create if you have a handful of potatoes and a half a cabbage in your fridge. These potato-dough pasties are super quick to make, and are light and satisfyingly soft and crunchy at the same time. You can stuff them with fillings from throughout the book, but here I offer a simple yet delicious filling of cabbage braised in tomato sauce, which can be made in advance. Serve *kartoplianyky* warm with a sour-cream-dressed cucumber and tomato salad, or enjoy a cheeky cold one straight out of the fridge.

Makes
12

500g (1lb 2oz) potatoes, peeled and cubed

180g (6½oz) plain (all-purpose) flour, plus extra for dusting

1 egg, beaten

a pinch of salt

vegetable oil, for frying

FOR THE FILLING

2 onions, thinly sliced

vegetable oil, for frying

400g (14oz) cabbage, shredded

1 tablespoon tomato purée

1 teaspoon sugar

1 tablespoon fennel seeds, toasted and crushed

2 tablespoons finely chopped dill

salt and black pepper to taste

Place the potatoes in a small saucepan of salted water, bring to the boil, then reduce the heat and simmer for 10–15 minutes. Drain and mash as well as you can. Let them cool completely before handling.

In a large bowl, mix the mashed potatoes with the flour, egg and salt, then knead into a ball. Let it rest while you prepare the filling.

Heat a little oil in a large frying pan and fry the onions with a pinch of salt over a medium heat for 10 minutes. Add the cabbage with another pinch of salt, and cook for another 10 minutes. Next, add the tomato purée, sugar and fennel seeds along with a splash of water to loosen up the paste, and thoroughly mix through until the cabbage is covered in the sauce. Cook over low heat for 5–7 minutes. Stir through the dill, take off the heat and let cool down.

Tip the dough onto a lightly floured surface and shape into a long sausage. Divide equally into eight balls, then pat each ball out into a flat disc, around 16cm (6¼in) in diameter. Make sure to dust the surface under each ball so that it doesn't stick.

Fill each disc with 2 heaped tablespoons of the cabbage mixture and pinch the tops to form an oblong shape, similar to the *piroshki* buns (see page 30).

When ready to cook, heat enough oil (4–6 tablespoons) for shallow-frying in a large pan (the exact amount will depend on the size of the pan) and fry on each side for 2–3 minutes. Place on paper towel to absorb excess oil before serving.

Potato Babka

For many, the word 'babka' brings to mind a gorgeous plaited bread, filled with chocolate and other delightful things. However, this *babka* is made out of potato and is more similar to a rösti. It is astonishing how just a handful of ingredients can produce something so satisfyingly delicious. As with many dishes in this book, it is hard to pinpoint its exact place of origin within Eastern Europe – Ashkenazi Jews have their version known as the potato *kugel*, in Ukraine a similar potato cake is called *borenchyk*, while the Poles and the Belarussians call it *babka*. The shape and cooking methods differ too: opt for a pan as I do here (like in Belarus) or a baking tin (Poland and Ukraine). When it comes to ingredients, you can keep it simple, as I do here, or add some fried bacon and/or mushrooms to the mix. The best part of the dish for me is the caramelised buttery onions that melt into the batter giving it a sweet, moist quality. Serve the babka warm with sour cream. Any leftovers can be reheated the next day in a pan.

Serves
4

- vegetable oil, for frying and greasing
- 2 onions, thinly sliced
- 20g (¾oz) salted butter
- 800g (1lb 12oz) potatoes, scrubbed
- 1 large egg
- 2 tablespoons sour cream, plus extra to serve
- 2 tablespoons plain (all-purpose) flour
- salt and black pepper to taste

Preheat the oven to 200°C (400°F).

In a large, ovenproof frying pan, fry the onions in a drizzle of oil with a generous pinch of salt over a medium heat for 12–15 minutes. Add the butter and continue cooking for a further 10 minutes.

In the meantime, grate the potatoes, skin and all, into a large bowl.

When the onions are done, tip them into the bowl with the grated potatoes. Add the egg, sour cream, flour and a generous pinch of salt and pepper.

Heat a little more oil in the same frying pan, tip the potato batter into it so that it starts sizzling straight away. Press it into the pan and place in the oven for 1 hour, until a delightful golden crust is formed. The *babka* might still feel a bit soft in the middle, which is fine, just let it sit for 10 minutes or so before serving.

Latkes

These medallions of crispy golden perfection are arguably the best-known items of Ashkenazi cuisine across the world. Traditionally made during one of the most important Jewish holidays, Hanukkah, they are a celebration of the miracle of oil, that allowed the Jews to rededicate the Jerusalem Temple, after their unlikely victory against a far more powerful enemy. Growing up in a Ukrainian-Jewish family in Russia, I have eaten these a countless number of times, but had never heard of the word *latkes* until I moved to the UK. Indeed, in Slavic-speaking Eastern Europe these are known as *oladki*, *draniki* or *deruny*. And in fact, the Yiddish name, *latkes*, derives from the Slavic word for fritters.

Commonly made with potatoes (from the 19th century onwards), these can also be made with other root vegetables (as they were prior to the1800s). The sky is your limit there – try a mix of beetroot and carrot or beetroot with sauerkraut. *Latkes* are traditionally served with apple sauce or sour cream. I honestly struggle to think of a more satisfying gastronomic experience than biting into a hot crispy potato fritter dipped in cooling, tangy sour cream. Here I offer a slight variation on the classic, but you can easily replace the sauerkraut with more potatoes if you don't have it available.

Makes
12

4 medium potatoes

1 onion, thinly sliced

8 heaped tablespoons Classic Sauerkraut (see page 184) or shop-bought

4 tablespoons plain (all-purpose) flour

2 large eggs

salt and black pepper to taste

vegetable oil for shallow-frying

FOR THE HERBED SOUR CREAM

200g (7oz) sour cream

handful of finely chopped dill

pinch of sea salt, to taste

Peel the potatoes and coarsely grate. Mix with the thinly sliced onion, and sprinkle with a pinch of salt.

Drain all the liquid from the mix using a paper towel or a muslin (cheesecloth).

Place into a large bowl. Squeeze the liquid out of the sauerkraut using the same method and add to the bowl along with the eggs and flour, and season with some salt and pepper. Make sure you reserve the sauerkraut liquid – use it in a salad dressing.

Heat enough oil for shallow-frying in a large frying pan (4–6 tablespoons, though the exact amount will depend on the size of the pan).

Shape 1–2 tablespoons of mixture into a flat fritter shape and place carefully into the pan. Fry over a medium high heat in small batches so as not to overcrowd the pan for 2–4 minutes on each side.

Remove and drain on a paper towel. Sprinkle with some salt and serve immediately with herbed sour cream, which you can make by mixing sour cream with the herbs and salt

Patatnik – Bulgarian Potato Pie

This dish comes from the Rhodope Mountains in Bulgaria, a region known for its glorious waxy potato variety, and could have been an identical twin of Potato Babka (see page 99) were it not for the addition of feta and mint, which remind us, in the most delicious way, of Bulgaria's proximity to the Balkans, Greece and Turkey.

Serves
8

- 800g (1lb 12oz) potatoes
- 1 large red onion, thinly sliced
- 2 garlic cloves, finely chopped
- 200g (7oz) feta, crumbled
- 1 teaspoon dried mint or 1 tablespoon finely chopped fresh mint
- 2 tablespoons finely chopped parsley
- 3 eggs, lightly beaten
- 20g (¾oz) butter
- salt and black pepper to taste

Preheat the oven to 180°C (350°F).

Peel and grate the potatoes. Wrap in paper towel or a muslin (cheesecloth) and squeeze out as much water as you can.

Tip the potatoes into a large bowl and mix with the onion, garlic, 150g (3½oz) of the feta and the herbs. Add the eggs and stir well.

Melt half the butter in a non-stick ovenproof frying pan over a medium-high heat, then tip in the potato mix – it should sizzle. Press the mixture into the pan. Fry on one side for 6–8 minutes, then cover the pan with a plate and flip the potato cake out.

Melt the remaining butter in the same pan and slide the cake off the plate back into the pan to cook it on the other side for 6–8 minutes.

Crumble the remaining feta on top then finish the pie in the oven for 15–20 minutes.

I love serving this with some Greek yoghurt and Carrot Tapenade (page 134), or with Smoky Carrot and Red Pepper Cream Cheese (page 136).

Kobete – Pryazovia Greek Meat and Potato Pie

I never knew about the presence of a Greek diaspora in the southern coastal areas of Ukraine until I came across the pastry chef and baker, Olga Koutseridi, on Instagram. Originally from Mariupol, Olga draws on her PhD as a historian to share not just recipes but the essential histories behind them, preserving important legacies of the Azov-sea area (Pryazovia) which has been greatly damaged since the Russian invasion in 2022. Here is Olga's family recipe in her own words:

'This recipe comes from my Greek Ukrainian grandmother, Eudokia; she learned it from her grandmother. This meat pie was reserved for special occasions such as holidays and communal celebrations. *Kobete* is a national dish of Crimean Tatars and Crimean Greeks. According to my grandmother, it was served for special guests that would visit Greek-Ukrainian villages all over Pryazovia. Traditionally the pastry for this pie is made using an incredibly laborious laminating process. I adapted this recipe to accommodate the busy home cook with the intention of making this pie more accessible and enjoyed more frequently! You can substitute lamb with ground beef, pork, or chicken.'

Serves
6–8

490g (1lb 1oz) puff pastry (2 sheets)

500g (1lb 2oz) potatoes, thinly sliced

2 teaspoons salt

1 egg, beaten, for brushing

1 teaspoon sesame seeds

1 teaspoon black sesame seeds

FOR THE FILLING

450g (1lb) minced (ground) lamb

400g (14oz) onions, peeled and finely diced

35g (1¼oz) coriander (cilantro), chopped

1 tablespoon ground cumin

1 teaspoon ground fenugreek (optional)

1 teaspoon salt

1 teaspoon cracked black pepper

TO SERVE

small bunches of fresh dill, coriander (cilantro) and spring onions (scallions), chopped

Preheat the oven to 200°C (400°F).

To make the filling, mix the lamb mince, onions, coriander, cumin, fenugreek (if using), and salt and pepper.

Roll out one of the pastry sheets into a large rectangle, approximately 27 x 38cm (10¾ x 15in), and no thicker than 1mm. Transfer the dough to a 23 x 33cm (9 x 13in) non-stick, rectangular baking tray (pan) pushing it into the sides. (It is important to have enough dough to cover the sides of the baking tray as you will need the extra dough for sealing the pie.)

Place half the potatoes in a single layer covering the bottom of the pie, season with salt, then spread the meat mixture evenly across the potatoes, again seasoning with salt. Cover the meat layer with the remaining potato slices and season with salt. Then take the second sheet of pastry and roll it out into a rectangle large enough to cover the top of the pie. Transfer the rolled-out pastry onto the pie and seal it around the edges.

Brush the top of the pie with the egg, sprinkle with the sesame seeds, and cut a cross in the middle of the pie to act as a vent. Bake on the middle shelf of the oven for 50 minutes to 1 hour, until the pastry is a golden brown colour. Serve hot, garnished with coriander, dill and lots of spring onions.

DUMPLINGS

CHAPTER FOUR

DUMPLINGS

Where and when exactly dumplings appeared on the table of *Homo sapiens* is unknown, but many sources say that the first documented evidence of dumpling-making and -eating is from China. This tradition then spread westward via the nomadic Turkic people from the Tatar-Mongol and Ottoman Empires, and this is how dumplings made their way into Eastern Europe. While the Turkic and Mongol dumplings would have been stuffed with mutton and fragrant spices, their Eastern European offspring flourished in all sorts of culinary directions, with pork and beef being the most common meat filling, and potatoes, mushrooms and cabbage the most frequent vegetarian filling. However, the true ingenuity of Eastern European dumplings came in the form of sweet fillings. Cherries, plums, apricots, wild strawberries, blueberries and other forest berries, as well as sweet curd cheeses. If there is a heaven, my version would be built entirely out of cherry dumplings with sweet sour cream!

While I love the idea of tracing all dumplings to some kind of primordial mother-dumpling another scenario is also possible. As the very idea of dumplings seems like common sense, it is fair to presume that many households across the globe at one point or another came up with the same idea of encasing food (perhaps leftovers) into soft dough and boiling it.

Although there is a rather delicious catalogue of other types of dumplings, such as the filling-less *kletski*, *halusky*, *kopytki* and *nokedli*, this chapter celebrates the kinds that boast scrumptious fillings. To me, there is something magical about this kind of dumpling. Perhaps it's the joy of revealing the filling, akin to that of unwrapping a gift. Or maybe it has something to do with my Ukrainian grandpa, Yuri, who read to me in abundance the fantastical stories of Mykola Hohol (known globally under his Russified name, Nikolai Gogol). In one of them, 'Christmas Eve', an evil sorcerer called Patsyuk had the superpower to make his *varenyky* dumplings fly out of a bowl and into his mouth, dipping themselves in sour cream along the way! This was the ultimate dream for me as a child! While I have no recipe for flying *varenyky* here, I nevertheless hope that the sheer variety of dumpling shapes and flavours in this chapter will enchant you for a lifetime!

Kreplach – Ashkenazi Dumplings in a Vegan Soup

Kreplach are pasta dumplings, filled with meat or vegetables and boiled in a broth. They are the Ashkenazi relatives of other types of Eastern European dumplings like the Ukrainian *varenyky* or the Polish *pierogi*. It is very likely that *kreplach* came to Central and Eastern Europe via the Italian Jews who began to resettle from the Sephardic (Spanish/Portuguese/Italian) communities to Eastern Europe via Germany starting in the 14th century. Some sources even suggest that *kreplach* were the original forefathers of Eastern European dumplings. Served on many Jewish holidays, they are a staple during the festival of Purim; some say the dumplings symbolise the revelation of Esther's Jewish identity, which helped save her people. Here I am offering the most universal vegetarian version, which can be easily made vegan or indeed with meat. As for the shape, you can come across a myriad. To me the classic *kreplach* is a triangle shape, but you can pinch the triangles' edges to make them look very similar to Italian tortellini to enhance their ancestral connection or opt for the half-moon shapes of their Ukrainian and Polish siblings.

Serves
4–6

FOR THE SIMPLE SOUP

vegetable oil, for frying

1 onion, diced

1 large carrot, peeled and grated

½ fennel, diced

2 celery sticks, thinly sliced

3–4 garlic cloves, finely chopped

1 tablespoon mixed dried herbs

¼ teaspoon turmeric

20g (¾oz) fresh dill and parsley, finely chopped

salt and black pepper

FOR THE DUMPLING DOUGH

300g (10½oz) plain (all-purpose) flour, plus extra for dusting

2 teaspoons dried dill

1 teaspoon salt

3 eggs

Start with the soup. In a large saucepan, heat the oil and fry all the vegetables, apart from the garlic, with a generous pinch of salt a medium heat for 20 minutes, or until softened and slightly caramelised. Add the garlic, dried herbs and turmeric and cook for another 2 minutes. Pour in 1 litre (4 cups) water, add a generous pinch of salt, bring to the boil, then reduce the heat and simmer for 15 minutes. When the time is up, add the fresh herbs and take the pan off the heat. Let the flavours infuse while you finish the rest.

To make the dumpling dough, mix the flour, dill and salt in a large bowl. In a separate bowl, beat the eggs with 80ml (2¾fl oz) water, then pour into the bowl with the dry ingredients. Start by mixing with a fork, then gradually work the mixture with your hands to form a dough. Knead the dough for 2 minutes, cover with cling film (plastic wrap), and let it rest in the fridge while you prepare the filling.

Place the potato in a large saucepan, cover with salted water, bring to the boil and cook until soft. Heat some oil in a frying pan and fry the onion with a pinch of salt over a medium heat for 15 minutes, or until caramelised. Tip into a bowl. Add a little more oil to the same pan and fry the mushrooms for 10 minutes. Tip into the bowl with the onion.

When the potato is ready, drain, add the butter, mash, then add to the bowl with the onion and mushrooms and mix well. It might seem like very little, but this is exactly how much you'll need for the filling.

FOR THE DUMPLING FILLING

1 large potato (weighing approx. 100g/3½oz), peeled and cubed

vegetable oil, for frying

1 onion, thinly sliced

200g (7oz) white button mushrooms, finely diced

20g (¾oz) butter

Dust a clean surface with some flour and work the dough for a few minutes to wake it up. Next, roll it out into a large rectangle. We are aiming for as thin a sheet as you possibly can produce. Trim off the edges to make an even rectangle (reserve the dough in the cling film), then cut the rectangle into even squares. You will probably get four vertically and seven or eight horizontally.

Have two lightly damp dish towels ready. Cover the squares with one, and reserve the other for finished dumplings. To shape the dumplings, pick up each square, fill it with a shy teaspoon of the filling and fold it into a triangle shape, pinching all edges closed. Place under the other towel, while you finish the rest.

Bring a large saucepan of water to the boil, then boil the dumplings for 5 minutes. Drain.

To serve, place around 4 dumplings into a soup bowl and top with a ladle of broth. Season with black pepper and tuck in while everything is steaming hot.

Polish Pierogi with Sauerkraut and Mushrooms

These dumplings are arguably the first thing that comes to mind when people are asked to name a Polish dish. Indeed, these plump beauties are a staple in Poland and can be considered more of a culinary genre rather than a specific dish. Just take a look at the brilliant cookbook *Pierogi* by Zuza Zak to marvel at the sheer variety of shapes and names these dumplings are known by. The more I delved into the history of this dish, the more I found myself falling down a rabbit hole into a magical world of dumplings that connects all Eastern European countries and branches out further into Italy, the Turkic world reaching all the way to China. This recipe could have been easily called *varenyky* – the Ukrainian equivalent – or *pirohy*, as they are known in Slovakia, as they are similar in shape and have similar culinary status in the food culture of each country. Here, I also add an optional topping of crispy onions and bacon, known as *skwarki*, *škvarky* or *shkvarky* in Poland, Slovakia and Ukraine, respectively.

Serves
4

FOR THE DOUGH

300g (10½oz) plain (all-purpose) flour, plus extra for dusting

1 teaspoon salt

2 eggs

100ml (3½fl oz) warm water

1 tablespoon vegetable oil

FOR THE FILLING

vegetable oil, for frying

1 onion, thinly sliced

200g (7oz) chestnut mushrooms, diced

150g (5½oz) Classic Sauerkraut (see page 184), or shop-bought, drained

1 bay leaf

1 teaspoon fennel seeds, lightly toasted and crushed

melted butter or sour cream

salt and black pepper, to taste

FOR THE TOPPING (OPTIONAL)

vegetable oil, for frying

20g (¾oz) pancetta

1 onion, finely chopped

To make the dough, mix the flour and salt in a large bowl. In a separate bowl, whisk the eggs with the warm water and oil, then pour into the bowl of dry ingredients. Start by mixing with a fork, then gradually work the mixture with your hands to form a dough. Knead it for 2 minutes, cover with cling film (plastic wrap), and rest in the fridge while you prepare the filling.

Heat the oil in a lidded frying pan and fry the onion with a pinch of salt over a medium heat for 8–10 minutes. Add the mushrooms and cook, with the lid on, until they have softened and released their liquid. Add the sauerkraut, bay leaf and fennel seeds, and continue to cook, covered, for 30 minutes, stirring occasionally. (Letting the sauerkraut catch a little on the bottom of the pan only enhances the richness of the flavours.) Take off the heat.

To make the *pierogi*, dust a clean surface with some flour and work the dough for a few minutes to wake it up. Next, roll it out into a large sheet of any shape, as thinly as you can. Using an upside-down mug or a pastry ring, cut out as many circles as you can, roughly 5–6cm (2–2½in) in diameter. Knead the off-cuts into a ball and place under cling film.

Add a tablespoon of the filling in the middle of each disc and pinch the edges firmly to create a half-moon shape. Keep the finished dumplings under a damp tea towel, while you make the rest of the *pierogi*.

To cook the *pierogi*, bring a large saucepan of salted water to the boil and cook in batches for 5 minutes, or until they float to the top. Use a slotted spoon to remove them and serve with melted butter or sour cream and lots of pepper.

If making the crispy pancetta and onion topping, fry the pancetta and onion in a frying pan with a pinch of salt for 20–30 minutes, or until deeply caramelised.

Kalduny – Belarussian Dumplings with Cabbage and Beef

My paternal grandfather, Arkadii, came from Dobruš, a small Belarussian town on the border with Ukraine and Russia, but he lived most of his life in the Russian Far East, and it was at their summer house there that he and my grandmother, Tamara, made the most delicious *kalduny* dumplings for us. The preparation was a ritual involving a large wooden tray and a special rounded knife with ornate wooden handles on both sides of the blade, which in my imagination resembled the stuff of folk legends. The fact that the word *kalduny* means 'sorcerers' in many Slavic languages only reinforced the aura of magic. This wonderful set can be approximated with a hachoir or mezzaluna, commonly used for chopping herbs. In this case, the rounded knife and tray were used for making the *kalduny* filling – meat, finely chopped by hand, together with onions, cabbage and dill. The filling was then encased in dough, to make giant half-moon shaped dumplings, boiled and served with lashings of melted butter and an extremely generous seasoning of black pepper. Other versions of *kalduny* can be found in Polish and Lithuanian cuisines (the dish itself originates from the Polish-Lithuanian Commonwealth of which modern-day Belarus was a part). Interestingly, a similar name for dumplings exists in Romanian – *colțunași* – which can be traced back to Italian calzone. This would certainly explain the shape and size of the Slavic fairytale sorcerers of my childhood.

Serves 4–6 (MAKES 40 LARGE DUMPLINGS)

1 x quantity Polish Pierogi dough (see page 115)

melted butter, to serve

FOR THE FILLING

1 large onion, thinly sliced

500–600g (1lb 2oz–1lb 5oz) cabbage, finely shredded using a mandoline

200g (7oz) minced (ground) beef or 300g (10½oz) mushrooms, very finely chopped

25g (1oz) dill, finely chopped

salt and black pepper, to taste

Place the onions and cabbage on a board and, using a large knife, chop them together to get a mince-like mixture. Place in a bowl with two generous pinches of salt and pepper, add the beef or mushrooms and the dill, and give everything a good mix with your hands.

Dust a clean surface with some flour and work the dough for a few minutes to wake it up, then roll it out into a large sheet of any shape, as thinly as you can.

Using an upside-down mug or a pastry ring, cut out as many circles as you can, roughly 9–10cm (3½–4in) in diameter. Knead the off-cuts into a ball and place under the cling film.

Place a heaped tablespoon of the filling in the middle of each disk and pinch the edges firmly to create a half-moon shape. Keep the finished dumplings under a damp tea towel, while you use up the rest of the dough and the filling.

To cook the dumplings, bring a large saucepan of salted water to the boil and cook in batches – 8 minutes for vegetable dumplings and 14 minutes for meat dumplings. Serve with melted butter and plenty of black pepper.

Tatar Manti with Carrots and Pumpkin

Manti are a signature dumpling of the Turkic world that are common across major parts of Muslim Central and West Asia, Southern Caucasus and parts of the Balkans. Varying in size, they can be served in their tiniest form in a soup or a rich sauce as in Turkish or Azerbaijani cuisines, or as palm-sized domes, steamed and served with a spicy tomato sauce, as in the cuisines of Central Asia, for example. Both meat and vegetarian versions are common, and the pinching techniques are emblematic of their native region. Tatar *manti* change their shape and size depending on the group that makes them: the Crimean Tatar manti are very similar to their Turkish neighbours (in fact in the Black Sea regions of Turkey these are called Tatar *böregi*), the Volga Tatar *manti* are identical to those served in the countries of Central Asia, while the Polish (or Lipka) Tatar manti are closer to East Asian *momos*. The shape often dictates the filling: the smaller the manti the more likely they will be filled with meat mince, while the larger varieties are stuffed with cubed vegetables (and chopped meat), and this is the version that I am offering here. A spicy red sauce is a more common condiment for these, but I am mixing things up a little and suggesting a Crimean Tatar-Turkish style garlicky yoghurt dip.

Serves
4–6

(MAKES 20 DUMPLINGS)

FOR THE DOUGH

1 egg

100ml (scant ½ cup) water

1 teaspoon salt

300g (10½oz) plain (all-purpose) flour, plus extra for dusting

FOR THE FILLING

1 onion, finely diced

200g (7oz) carrots, peeled and finely cubed

200g (7oz) butternut squash, peeled and finely cubed

1 tablespoon ground cumin

1 tablespoon ground coriander

1–2 teaspoons fine sea salt

1 tablespoon sunflower oil

20g (¾oz) butter, cut into small cubes

To make the dough, beat the egg with the water in a bowl. Sift the salt and flour into a large bowl. Add the wet ingredients to the bowl with the flour and knead until a firm ball is shaped. Tip out onto a lightly floured surface and knead for 8–10 minutes until the dough is elastic. Leave to rest under a damp tea towel, while you prepare the filling.

Combine all the ingredients for the filling except the butter in a bowl.

Next, shape the dumplings. On a clean surface dusted with flour, roll out the dough into a thin sheet – it is best to use a pasta machine here, if you can, otherwise aim for 2–3mm (⅛in) thick using a rolling pin.

Cut the sheet into 8–10cm (3¼–4in) squares. Reuse the cut-offs to make as many squares as you can. Fill each square with a heaped tablespoon of the filling and add a little cube of butter in the middle.

Sealing the *manti* is a skill: start by pressing any two opposite corners together above the filling. Then take the other two corners and press them together over the previous ones. Now you have a square-shaped parcel. Press the two corners of the parcel together on one side, and then repeat on the other side, as if making little handles for the parcel on both sides. *Voila!*, you have your Central Asian-style Tatar *manti* shape!

Prepare your steaming arrangement by setting water in a medium-large saucepan to boil and generously oiling the insert basket/rack so that the dumplings don't stick together.

FOR THE SUMAC-YOGHURT SAUCE

200ml (7fl oz) yoghurt

1 garlic clove, finely grated

a pinch of chilli flakes

a pinch of sumac

salt and black pepper to taste

sprigs of dill, to serve

Make a batch of *manti* that comfortably fits into the steamer without being overcrowded and get them cooking while you finish shaping the rest. Cover with a lid and steam for 25–30 minutes, then carefully remove the *manti* from the basket, drizzle with a little melted butter or oil, and cover with foil to keep warm while you finish the rest.

Make the sauce. In a small bowl, mix the yoghurt with the garlic, chilli powder and sumac. Season to taste.

Serve the *manti* on a large platter drizzled with the sauce and garnished with sprigs of dill. It's a real show-stopper!

Tatar Khanum – Steamed Rose-Shaped Dumplings with Vegetables

Khanum are rose-shaped dumplings, popular across Central Asia, that made their way into Tatar cuisine via the migration of people between Eastern Europe and Asia. Traditionally made with beef, this vegetarian recipe was given to me by Firuza Yusupova, a pastry chef of Jewish-Tatar origin. It feels so significant knowing that a special family recipe will live on in this book – especially one that goes back several generations. It came from Firuza's grandmother (*babulia*), Karima, who lived between Bashkortostan (in the Eastern European part of Russia) and Samarkand (Uzbekistan). This is such a beautiful and delicious example of how a family's history of migration can be told through food.

Traditionally these were served with a homemade Tatar sour-milk drink called *katyk*, which granny Karima made herself, but you can use shop-bought kefir or very runny yoghurt.

Makes 15–20
Serves 4–6

FOR THE DOUGH

1 egg

100ml (3½fl oz) water

300g (10½oz) plain (all-purpose) flour

pinch of salt

FOR THE FILLING

50g (1¾oz) butter

1 onion, finely diced

2 small carrots, peeled and finely diced

2 potatoes, peeled and finely diced

½ small cabbage, finely diced

1 teaspoon ground cumin

salt and black pepper to taste

FOR THE DRIZZLING SAUCE

1 garlic clove, finely chopped (or more to taste)

1 tablespoon finely chopped parsley

200ml (7fl oz) kefir or very runny yoghurt

To make the dough, beat the egg in a bowl with the water. In a separate bowl, mix together the flour and salt, then add the wet ingredients. Mix together to form a dough. Knead the dough for a few minutes – it will be quite firm and dry. Cover with cling film and let it rest while you prepare the filling.

Melt the butter in a heavy-based pan or casserole (Dutch oven) over a medium heat and fry the onion for 3–5 minutes. Stir in the carrots and potatoes, and cook for another 5 minutes. You might want to add a splash of water here. Finally, add the cabbage, and allow it to soften a little. All the vegetables need to retain some bite.

Season generously with salt and pepper and add the cumin. Take off heat, and let the filling cool down while you deal with the dough.

Tip the dough out onto a lightly floured surface and knead for a few minutes to wake it up. Divide the dough into three parts, leaving the others wrapped while you work with one.

For the rolling of the dough, although not traditional, I would recommend using a pasta machine. Roll out each dough ball into a thin sheet – run the dough through the machine a few times until you get to the medium-small setting (number 5 or 6) on the machine. Then, using a glass, cut out as many discs, 7–8cm (2¾–3½in) in diameter, as you can.

Place four discs in a line so that they overlap almost by half. Press them down to stick them together. Take 1 heaped tablespoon of the filling and place into a thin line in the middle of the dough discs. Fold

the dough over at the top, but do not seal the edges. Then, roll the dough sideways so that the unsealed edge with the filling remains at the top. Place the dumpling on its bottom side, with the unsealed edge still at the top. Keep the finished dumplings under a damp tea towel while you finish the rest.

To cook the dumplings, prepare your steaming arrangement by setting water in a saucepan to boil and generously oiling the insert basket or rack so that the dumplings don't stick together.

Place a batch of dumplings into the steamer that fits comfortably without being overcrowded. Cover with a lid and steam for 25–30 minutes. Carefully remove from the steamer, drizzle with a little melted butter or oil and cover with foil to keep warm while you finish steaming the remaining dumplings.

Mix the ingredients for the drizzling sauce together in a bowl. Adjust the garlic and seasoning to taste, then pour over the steaming dumplings before tucking in with your hands.

Udmurt Dumplings with Beetroot and Raspberry

Udmurts (from Permic for 'meadow people') are an ethnic group from the Eastern European part of Russia, who reside in the region between Tatarstan, Bashkortostan and the Ural Mountains. They come from Finno-Ugric lineage and are ethnically related to the Finns and Hungarians. Their food, although heavily influenced by the standardised Soviet diet, is full of unique and fascinating flavour combinations, and dishes like pies and dumplings are a regional staple. In fact, dumplings are so crucial to Udmurt culture that a 4-metre high monument depicting a giant dumpling perched on the end of a fork was erected in the region's capital, Izhevsk, in 2004. I'd love a miniature version for my kitchen shelf, wouldn't you?

Serves
4

1 x quantity Polish Pierogi dough (page 115)

FOR THE FILLING

90g (3¼oz) ready-cooked beetroot (beet)

1 tablespoon light brown sugar, or to taste

115g (4oz) fresh raspberries

TO SERVE

melted unsalted butter

light brown sugar

Grate the beetroot, drain and discard the juices, then mix in a bowl with the sugar. Add the raspberries, mixing gently with a fork to mash the raspberries a little, then taste and adjust the sweetness to your liking.

Next, shape the dumplings. Dust a clean surface with some flour and work the dough for a few minutes to wake it up. Then, roll it out into a large sheet of any shape, as thinly as you can. Using an upside-down mug or a pastry ring, cut out as many circles as you can, roughly 8cm (3¼in) in diameter. Knead the off-cuts into a ball and place under cling film.

Place a heaped tablespoon of the filling in the middle of each disc and pinch the edges firmly to create a half-moon shape. You can press them with the back of a fork to create a lovely frill effect. Keep the finished dumplings under a damp tea towel while you shape the rest.

To cook the dumplings, bring a large saucepan of salted water to the boil and cook in batches for 5 minutes, or until they float to the top. Remove with a slotted spoon and serve drizzled with melted butter and a sprinkle of sugar.

CARROT

CHAPTER FIVE

CARROT

Please excuse me while I attempt a culinary-sartorial metaphor: carrots are a bit like handbags. They may be used simply as a commodity to carry other stuff or they can be a statement centrepiece that brings the whole look together. On the one hand, there are a myriad of dishes where carrots are used as a carrier ingredient, a silent hero that endows recipes with the right amount of sweetness and earthiness. On the other, carrot can be a champion ingredient, claiming all of the much-deserved attention. For me, carrot is the only vegetable in the book that became an acquired taste as I grew up. Unless it was the Koryo-Saram spicy pickled carrots, or grated carrots mixed with sugary sour cream, I didn't want to come anywhere near the stuff. Chunks of boiled carrots in the soup or steamed carrots inside a bun? I'd be looking for the nearest emergency exit! Perhaps a bit like sprouts, it's all about how you cook them. These days, I can't exist without carrots in my kitchen. Grated into a slaw, ribboned and dressed with yoghurt and lemon juice, or sautéed in a pan with finely diced onion – this is my home! I feel grounded and delighted in the anticipation of a comforting meal to come.

The carrot's history starts in Persia and Central Asia, and this is not surprising, given just how many amazing carrot dishes can be found in the cuisines of that region. In this book you will find many recipes with carrots belonging to Tatar cuisine, which itself stems from and is part of the Turkic culinary culture. Over the centuries, carrots made their way to and across Europe, becoming a trusted friend.

Carrot's natural sweetness lends itself beautifully to desserts – grated into cake batter or turned into sweet fritters with cottage cheese and sultanas (golden raisins). And that very sweetness makes it an equally fantastic ingredient in recipes for ferments, of which there are plenty in this book.

Carrot Tapenade

A carrot relish is often used to accompany white fish in Eastern European cuisine, for example the carrot topping of the Ashkenazi gefilte fish, known as *yarmulka*, or the Polish cod and carrot dish called *ryba po grechku*. Another equally popular type of vegetable dip or relish is commonly known as 'caviar', aubergine one being the most popular. So, taking the best of both culinary traditions, I have created this smoky, tangy and sweet carrot tapenade. Enjoy with a crusty baguette as part of a *zakuski* spread or charcuterie platter, inside a cheese toastie (grilled cheese) or on top of a slice of rye bread smothered with cream cheese. This tapenade needs a day in the fridge to develop some oomph, so make it in advance.

Serves
6–8

vegetable oil, for frying

1 onion, thinly sliced

1 red (bell) pepper, thinly sliced

4 carrots, peeled and grated

1–2 garlic cloves, finely chopped

2 tablespoons tomato purée (paste)

2 teaspoons caster (superfine) sugar

1 teaspoon smoked paprika

½ teaspoon chilli powder or hot paprika (optional)

1 tablespoon white wine vinegar

2 tablespoons chopped dill

salt and black pepper, to taste

Heat a little oil in a lidded frying pan and cook the onion and pepper with a pinch of salt on a medium-low heat for 20 minutes, stirring occasionally. Add the carrots and cook for another 15 minutes, adding more oil if needed. Add the garlic, stir through, then add the tomato purée, 4 tablespoons of water to loosen it up, and the sugar. Cover and cook for 8 minutes.

Take off the heat and stir in the paprika, vinegar and dill. Taste for seasoning and adjust as needed. Let it cool down completely before transferring into a glass jar. Store in the fridge overnight before serving.

Smoky Carrot and Red Pepper Cream Cheese

Originally this recipe was inspired by a paprika cheese spread known as *liptauer* or *körözött* in Austria, Slovakia and Hungary. But as I looked into its variations, I found a recipe from Hungarian Romani cuisine called *ciganyturo*, which uses sautéed carrots, red (bell) peppers and onions, generously seasoned with smoked paprika. While *ciganyturo* uses local cottage cheese, I have experimented with different dairy bases in its absence, and could not be happier with the result I share below. Try it with rye bread, pita or Turkish *pide* bread, which I believe would be the closest equivalent to the traditional Romani bread called *bodag*.

Serves
6–8

- olive oil, for frying
- ½ onion, thinly sliced
- 1 red (bell) pepper, thinly sliced
- 2 carrots, peeled and grated
- 1 heaped teaspoon smoked paprika
- 250g (9oz) full-fat cream cheese (or 125g/4½oz feta and 125g/4½oz cream cheese)
- salt, to taste

Heat a drizzle of oil in a frying pan and fry the onion, pepper and carrots with a pinch of salt over a medium heat for 25–30 minutes until they start to caramelise. Take off the heat and mix in the paprika. Let it cool down a little.

Transfer the vegetables to a food processor with the cream cheese. You can use a hand blender and a tall narrow jar for this, too. Blend until smooth, then adjust the seasoning to your liking. If the mixture is too runny, place it in the fridge for a few hours to firm up before serving.

Knishes – Ashkenazi Buns with Caramelised Carrots and Chicken

Thanks to this book, Ashkenazi *knishes* have become dear friends on my table. I have tried various classic fillings (see page 94) and I really wanted to create one that I could call my own. Dipping my toes again in my favourite flavour combo of carrots, prunes and chicken (yes, I am a hopeless *tzimmes* obsessive), I have created something juicy, crispy, sweet and salty at once. If I struggled previously to cap my consumption of these buns, all hope was lost when I baked a bunch with this filling.

Makes
14

1 x quantiy *knishes* dough (see page 94)

FOR THE FILLING

4 skinless and boneless chicken thighs

vegetable oil, for frying

2 onions, thinly sliced

3–4 carrots, peeled and grated

1 teaspoon caraway seeds, toasted and roughly pounded

8 pitted prunes, finely chopped

15–20g (½–¾oz) butter

1 small bunch of dill or parsley, finely chopped

salt to taste

Season the chicken thighs with salt on both sides. Heat some oil in a lidded frying pan and, over a medium-high heat, fry the chicken for 10 minutes on each side until golden. Remove from the pan and set aside.

Add the onions, carrots and a pinch of salt to the pan, and fry over a medium heat for 20 minutes, or until caramelised. Lower the heat, add the caraway seeds and prunes and continue cooking while you chop the chicken into bite-sized chunks. Return the chicken to the pan, add the butter and stir through. Take off the heat and let it rest under the lid and cool down.

Preheat the oven to 180°C (350°F).

Divide the dough in half. Put one half in a bowl and cover with cling film (plastic wrap) while you work the other half. Dust a surface with flour and roll out the dough into large rectangle, as thin as you can. Some traditional Jewish recipes recommend as thin as a tablecloth. Trim off the wonky edges.

Take half the filling and shape it into a log across the longest side of the dough rectangle, roughly 1cm (½in) from the edge. Pull the dough over the filling and continue rolling until the log is lying in front of you, seam-side down. Keep rolling it back until the filling is evenly distributed and the seam is not as pronounced. Pinch the ends and cut off any excess dough.

Divide the log into equal segments roughly 6–7cm (2½–2¾in) long: make subtle incisions with the blunt end of a knife, but don't cut all the way through. Next, use the edge of your hand to cut through the incisions and seal each bun that way. Pick up each *knish*, seal the bottom and the top and squash it a little to give it that distinct *knish* shape.

Place on a baking sheet, leaving a bit of space in between, and make a little indentation in the middle of each *knish* with your thumb. Brush generously with egg wash and bake for 45 minutes, rotating halfway through.

These taste best served warm or at room temperature.

Pearl Barley Tabbouleh with Roasted Carrots and Walnuts

Ever since I discovered the wonders of *tzimmes* (see page 147), I simply cannot look at carrots without thinking of all the inexhaustible variations of flavours made possible by that wondrous carrot-centric Jewish dish. This recipe is sort of an improvisation on various dishes of the Ashkenazi cuisine – *tzimmes*, of course, and *cholent*, a pearl barley and root vegetable stew, with a nod to the Mizrahi cuisine in the way the dish is presented as a tabbouleh salad rather than a stew. The result is a complex, fragrant dish with real bite and substance to it.

Serves
4–6

120g (4oz) pearl barley

10g (¼oz) salted butter

1kg (2lb 4oz) carrots, chopped into bite-sized chunks

2 red onions, cut into wedges

2 tablespoons vegetable oil

1 tablespoon runny honey

zest and juice of 1 small orange

50g (3¼oz) walnuts

1 tablespoon coriander seeds

1 tablespoon caraway seeds

30g (1oz) dried apricots, the soft plump kind

2 tablespoons chopped parsley

2 tablespoons chopped dill

sea salt flakes

FOR THE SALAD DRESSING

2 tablespoons unrefined sunflower oil

juice of ½ lemon

1 tablespoon apple cider vinegar

1 teaspoon clear honey

Preheat the oven to 200°C (400°F).

Cook the pearl barley according to the packet instructions. When ready, drain and stir in the salted butter.

In a bowl, mix together the oil, honey, orange zest and juice. Toss the carrots and the onions around in the bowl and place them on a baking tray (pan), pouring in any remaining marinade. Sprinkle generously with sea salt flakes. Roast in the oven for 40–45 minutes.

Meanwhile, heat a dry frying pan and toast the walnuts over a medium high heat for 5 minutes until they turn brown in places. Tip onto a chopping board, allow to cool a little, then roughly chop. Using the same pan, toast the coriander and caraway seeds for 5–8 minutes, then pound them roughly in a mortar and pestle. Roughly chop the apricots.

Make the dressing by mixing all the ingredients together with a couple of pinches of sea salt flakes until the honey and salt dissolve. To assemble, put the cooked barley and vegetables into a large bowl, add the apricots, walnuts, toasted seeds, herbs and the dressing. Gently mix together.

Chiboreki – Crimean Tatar Flatbreads with Lentils and Carrots

Chiboreki is a traditional, and the most widely acclaimed, dish of the Crimean Tatars. Popular all over Eastern Europe, the Caucasus, Russia and Central Asia, they are often called *chebureki*, while their original Turkic name is *çibörek*. Traditionally made with minced (ground) meat and onion, my recipe features spiced lentils and carrots, as I took inspiration from cuisines of different Turkic areas, such as Central Asia and Turkey. The key is to spread the filling thinly; this makes for a flat-shaped dough parcel. These must be consumed hot with a side of kefir, ayran or any other tangy yoghurty drink.

Makes
10–12

FOR THE DOUGH

300g (10½oz) plain (all-purpose) flour, plus extra for dusting

150ml (5½fl oz) just-boiled water

2 tablespoons vegetable oil

1 teaspoon salt

FOR THE FILLING

vegetable oil, for frying

3 carrots, peeled and grated

1 onion, diced

2 garlic cloves, finely chopped

1 teaspoon ground coriander

1 teaspoon ground cumin

½ teaspoon smoked paprika

½ teaspoon cracked black pepper

120g (4½oz) dried green lentils

1 bay leaf

1 large handful of coriander (cilantro) leaves, roughly chopped

squeeze of lemon

salt, to taste

500ml (2 cups) vegetable oil, for deep-frying

Place the flour into a large bowl. In a separate bowl, mix the just-boiled water with the oil and salt. Add the wet mixture to the bowl of flour. Using a fork to start with, stir to bring the dough together. When cool enough to handle, knead the dough with your hands – first in the bowl and then directly on a lightly floured work surface.

Work the dough by pressing it into the work surface and then rolling it away for 5 minutes, or until it comes together into a smooth ball. Wrap in cling film (plastic wrap) and leave to rest for 20 minutes.

Heat the oil in a casserole or large lidded frying pan. Fry the carrots, onions and garlic over a medium heat with a pinch of salt and all the spices for 10–15 minutes, or until soft and caramelised. Next, add the lentils, a pinch of salt and the bay leaf. Give everything a good stir and cover with enough water to evenly submerge the lentils. Cook for 20 minutes, stirring occasionally and adding a bit more water if needed, until the lentils are soft.

Take off the heat, add the coriander and a squeeze of lemon and taste for seasoning, adding more if necessary. Let it cool down while you get back to your dough. The lentils be made in advance and kept overnight.

Tip the dough onto a lightly floured surface and wake it up a little by working it for a minute. Divide it into 10 balls, about 55g (2oz) each, then roll each ball into a large, thin disc, 15–18cm (6–7in) in diameter.

Place 2 tablespoons of the filling into the middle of each disc, spread it thinly and fold the dough over in half to make a half-moon shape. Press the edges very tightly and flatten the filling in the middle so that it spreads evenly throughout. You can use a fluted pastry wheel or push the back of a fork flat into the edge of the dough to make a 'frill'.

Heat the vegetable oil in a large frying pan. The oil needs to be hot enough that the *chebureki* start sizzling as soon as they are lowered into the oil, but not so hot that it is smoking. Fry for 1 minute on one side, and 45 seconds on the other until golden brown.

Drain on a paper towel to absorb extra oil and consume ASAP.

Carrot and Lentil Soup from the Torah

When I was putting together a list of recipes for this chapter, I knew I wanted to include a carrot and lentil soup for no particular reason other than its deliciousness. I have found some recipes in Hungarian and Romanian cuisines, but while they got full marks on flavour, they lacked in story. And, in my view, a good recipe is indeed one with a story behind it. Then one day, I came across a passage from the Torah that is said to have inspired a recipe for a lentil soup in Ashkenazi cuisine, known as *linzen*. In this story, we meet two brothers Esau and Jacob (the forefather of the people of Israel), who change the fate of the Jewish people over a bowl of lentil soup. Esau comes home after a long day of hunting, famished and exhausted, to find his brother cooking a lentil stew – he calls it *ha-adom ha-adom hazeh*, literally 'that red stuff'. However, Jacob only agrees to share the food with his brother if Esau agrees to give up his birthright. As the text says: 'Jacob then gave Esau bread and lentil stew; he ate and drank and he rose and went away. Thus did Esau spurn the birthright.' There are versions of this soup in Jewish Sephardi and Ashkenazi cuisines, and the recipe I have here is an improvisation on various Eastern European flavours. It *is* really good, but I would not encourage you to use it to blackmail your relatives.

Serves
4

vegetable oil, for frying

1 onion, diced

4 carrots, peeled and diced

2 celery stalks, chopped

2 teaspoons ground coriander

2 teaspoons smoked paprika

2 teaspoons dried marjoram

2 tablespoons tomato purée (paste)

1 teaspoon honey

100ml (3½fl oz) just-boiled water

1 large potato, peeled and diced

250g (9oz) red lentils

500ml (17fl oz) vegetable or chicken stock

2 bay leaves

½ lemon

salt, to taste

generous pinch of dried chilli flakes

crusty bread, to serve (optional)

Heat the oil in a large saucepan and add the onion, carrots, celery, coriander, paprika, marjoram and a large pinch of salt. Sauté over a medium heat for 5–8 minutes until softened.

In a cup, stir the tomato purée and honey into the hot water, then add to the pan. Let it simmer for 2–3 minutes.

Add the lentils, stock and bay leaves to the pan, bring to the boil, then reduce the heat to a simmer for 30 minutes until the lentils are tender and falling apart. Squeeze in the lemon and drop it into the pot. Allow to simmer for a further 10 minutes.

You can serve the soup as is or opt for a chunky/semi-smooth consistency. For the latter, quickly run a stick blender through the pan, making sure to discard the lemon and the bay leaves first, puréeing it just enough to leave some texture.

To serve the soup, add a generous pinch of chilli flakes to each bowl and, if you like, a hefty chunk of crusty white bread on the side to mop up all the goodness.

Hungarian Goulash

Goulash can be likened to borsch in the sheer diversity of opinions on what constitutes 'an authentic version', its iconic status within the country and the level of confusion as to what it actually is that prevails in the countries outside of Eastern Europe. Generally speaking, the word 'goulash' is often used to describe any Eastern European stew of beef in a red sauce. And, indeed, there are a few dishes under that name in the cuisine of the region. For example, the Czech and Slovak goulash (*gulás)* is a stew of beef in a rich tomato gravy served with bread dumplings. However, in Hungary, goulash (known as *gulyás leves*) refers to a meat and (root) vegetable soup. *Gulyás leves* has a sibling, called *bogrács gulyás,* which is identical in content but is cooked outside on an open fire in a large cauldron called a *bogrács* (a similar soup exists in Ukrainian and Romanian cuisines, or rather the cuisines of those regions that were part of the Austro–Hungarian Empire). If you are after a traditional Hungarian stew, however, you need to look for *pörklöt* or *paprikash* and I will delve into these later in the book.

Serves
4

---

vegetable oil, for frying

1 onion, diced

500g (1lb 2oz) stewing beef, diced

1 teaspoon whisky or brandy (optional)

2 large tomatoes, cut into cubes, or 1 x 400g (14oz) tin chopped tomatoes

1 tablespoon tomato purée (paste)

1 teaspoon caster (superfine) sugar

4 garlic cloves, finely chopped

2 heaped teaspoons paprika

1 teaspoon caraway seeds

1.5 litres (51fl oz/6 cups) water or beef stock

2 bay leaves

4 carrots peeled and cut into bite-sized chunks

4 potatoes peeled and cut into bite-sized chunks

2 red (bell) pepper, cut into cubes

1 large bunch of parsley, finely chopped

salt and black pepper, to taste

crusty bread, to serve

Heat the oil in a large saucepan or deep casserole (Dutch oven) and fry the onion with a pinch of salt over a medium heat for 10 minutes, until softened. Add the beef, season lightly with salt, and brown on all sides. Add the whisky (if using), increase the heat and cook, stirring, for 1 minute.

Next, add the tomatoes, tomato purée, sugar and garlic. Give it a good stir. You might want to add a splash of water to loosen, and another pinch of salt. Stir in the paprika and the caraway seeds followed by the water (or stock) and bay leaves. Bring to the boil and cook over a medium heat for 40 minutes, or until the meat is tender.

Add the carrots, potatoes and pepper, and cook for another 20 minutes, or until cooked through. Taste and adjust the seasoning where needed, then throw in the parsley.

Serve with chunky bread and a glass of Hungarian Riesling.

Tzimmes – Ashkenazi Carrot, Beef and Prune Stew

A classic of Eastern European Jewish cuisine, this dish is a bit of a culinary shapeshifter. When I asked my Ashkenazi friends and acquaintances about it, I always got a different answer. Some say it's a meat stew, others call it a dessert, and quite often it's referred to as a side dish, which does make sense given the etymology of the word (from German *zuomuose* for 'side dish.') The one thing everyone agrees on is that *tzimmes* contains carrots, prunes and honey, and is eaten at Rosh Hashanah to symbolise the anticipation of a sweet year ahead. *Tzimmes* originated in the German Ashkenazi community during the Middle Ages, and travelled over to a then more religiously tolerant Poland in the 16th century, when antisemitism was rampant in Western Europe. The dish made its way around the world with waves of Jewish migration, starting in the 18th century, as antisemitic violence washed over Eastern Europe too. Today you can find local recipes for *tzimmes* in Mexico, Argentina, USA and the Balkans, where fruits like mango and pineapples are added, as well as beans and pulses and a rainbow of different spices. Researching the myriad of recipes I began to understand why the Yiddish expression *machan a tzimmes* or 'to fuss over' came about. Finally, I have decided to opt for the simplest yet most delicious version of the dish – a meat stew with carrots and prunes. This is definitely a Sunday lunch type of dish, as the overall cooking and preparation time comes to 3 hours. But the joy of tucking into the rich, sweet, smoky stew, is worth all the effort (or shall I say fuss?).

Serves
4–6

vegetable oil, for frying

500g (1lb 2oz) stewing beef, cut into chunks

2 onions, cut into chunks

8 carrots, peeled and cut into chunks

6 potatoes, peeled and cut into chunks

4 bay leaves

100g (3½oz) pitted prunes, roughly chopped

700ml (scant 3 cups) beef stock

1 tablespoon honey

2 teaspoons garlic powder

salt and black peppe,r to taste

1 small bunch of parsley

Note: For a vegetarian version, omit the beef, and add two extra carrots and two potatoes to make up the volume.

Preheat the oven to 160°C (320°F).

Heat a little oil in a casserole (Dutch oven) or ovenproof, lidded frying pan and fry the beef with a pinch of salt and pepper over a medium-high heat for about 10 minutes until browned on all sides. Remove from the pan and set aside.

Throw in the onions and carrots and coat them in the oil. Season with salt and pepper and fry for about 6 minutes, stirring occasionally, letting it brown in places.

Take off the heat. Return the beef to the casserole and mix well with the vegetables. Add the potatoes, the bay leaves and the prunes. Try to scatter them equally around the casserole.

In a jug (pitcher), mix the stock with the honey and garlic powder. Pour this into the casserole, cover and cook in the oven for 2½ hours.

Serve with a scattering of chopped parsley and enjoy immediately.

Tatar Pilaw

Rice and root vegetables are a staple in many Turkic cuisines, and the Tatar one is not an exception. *Pilaw* or *pilau* is a dish of meat, root vegetables (mainly carrots) and grains common across Central Asia, Persia and the Caucasus, which has become very popular in parts of Eastern Europe where the different branches of the Tatar tribes have settled. *Pilaw* is a real celebratory dish, where the meat plays a special part. However, vegetarian versions are also common and here I offer my own take on the classic flavours relying on the mighty carrot to deliver the flavour and texture, and it doesn't disappoint. This recipe feeds 8–10 because a real *pilaw* is always something of a feast. You can, though, easily halve all the ingredients for a weeknight meal.

Serves
8–10

800g (1lb 12oz) arborio, long grain or basmati rice

50ml (1¾fl oz) vegetable oil

2 large onions, sliced

300g (11oz) carrots, peeled and cut into 2cm (1in) cubes

1 litre (34fl oz/4 cups) vegetable stock

pinch of saffron threads

300g (11oz) butternut squash, cut into 2cm (1in) cubes

1 x 400g (14oz) tin chickpeas (garbanzos), drained and rinsed

2 teaspoons cumin seeds, toasted and roughly pounded

1 teaspoon ground coriander

½ teaspoon chilli powder

½ teaspoon ground black pepper

1 tablespoon barberries

1 large garlic bulb

25g (1oz) salted butter, cut into 6–8 chunks

small bunch each of parsley and coriander (cilantro)

Rinse the rice under tepid water until the water runs clear. Leave to soak in a bowl of water while you prepare the rest of the dish.

Heat the oil in a large casserole (Dutch oven) or lidded frying pan and fry the onions with a pinch of salt for 10 minutes over a medium heat until softened. Add the carrots and fry for 5–8 minutes until soft, stirring occasionally.

In a small bowl, mix a tablespoon of the stock with the saffron, then set aside to infuse.

Add the squash and chickpeas to the casserole together with all the spices, the barberries and a pinch of salt. Mix well. Add some of the stock, just enough to cover the vegetables, then pour in the saffron-infused stock and give everything a gentle mix. Drain and add the rice, mix gently, and make a hole in the middle where you will place the whole bulb of garlic. Now pour in more stock, enough so that it comes up 1cm (½in) above the rice level. You may also want to add another pinch of salt here.

Cover and simmer over a low heat for 30–35 minutes. Take off the heat, make 6–8 holes in the rice around in a circle and insert the butter chunks. Let the dish rest under the lid for about 10 minutes. Pop the garlic cloves out of their skins – they will now have metamorphosed into soft, sweet, pungent flavour bombs. Serve with a platter of fresh herbs on the side.

Kapusta

Carrot, Honey and Twarog Fritters

Cooking with sweet cottage cheese is one of the best traditions of Eastern European cuisine. These little sweet cottage cheese patties, known as *syrniki*, from the Slavic word *syr* for (cottage) cheese, make up the bulk of happy childhood memories for so many. I was always sure that this cooking idea was distinctly Eastern European in origin, but then, of course, there is no such thing as 'authentic' or 'distinct' when it comes to a phenonmenon so intricate as cooking. I think I actually said 'No!' out loud when I came across a passage, in Leah Koenig's brilliant encyclopaedia of Jewish cooking, which explained that sweet cottage cheese fritters entered Eastern Europe via Italian Jews, whose cuisine had a staple of ricotta and honey fritters from the 15th century onwards. I often substitute Eastern European twarog with ricotta when cooking *syrniki* in the UK, and previously thought it second best, but, as it turns out, it's in fact the ancestral ingredient! It goes without saying that you can replace twarog with ricotta here.

Makes
10–12

- 50g (1¾oz) unsalted butter
- 2 medium carrots, peeled and grated
- 2–3 tablespoons honey, or to taste
- 200g (7oz) twarog (or ricotta)
- 2 eggs, beaten
- 1 tablespoon sugar
- 1 scant teaspoon baking powder
- a pinch of salt
- 6 tablespoons plain (all-purpose) flour
- 2 tablespoons raisins, pre-soaked in 20ml (1½ tablespoons) rum (optional)
- grated zest of ½ lemon
- vegetable oil, for shallow-frying
- icing (powdered) sugar, for dusting
- crème fraîche, to serve

Melt the butter in a frying pan over medium-low heat and add the carrots and honey. Cook, stirring, for 10 minutes.

Mix the twarog, eggs, sugar, baking powder, salt, flour, raisins and lemon zest in a large bowl.

When the carrots are soft, remove from the heat and allow to cool. Add the carrots to the flour mixture, stirring to combine.

Heat enough oil for shallow-frying (about 4–6 tablespoons) in a large frying pan. Scoop two heaped tablespoons of the mixture directly into the hot oil and pat it down with the back of a spoon to form a fritter. There is no need to strive for perfection in shape, the more rustic they look, the better. Fry on each side on a medium high heat for 4 minutes.

Remove with a slotted spoon and let rest on a paper towel to absorb excess oil. Dust with a little icing sugar and serve with some crème fraîche.

A Tzimmes Carrot Cake

This recipe is pure invention, born out of the golden rule: as long as you have carrots and prunes, you can make a delicious dish and feature *tzimmes* in its name.

While I had initially shied away from trying the sweet version of the iconic Ashkenazi dish as I still could not quite put my finger on what a sweet carrot and prune stew would actually turn out to be, I had a good feeling about turning these delightful ingredients into a cake, and delving into the beautiful array of warming spices that the sweet *tzimmes* recipes often call for. So here you have it – a carrot cake with prunes, apricots, ginger and cinnamon. Grab a tub of sour cream and tuck in!

Makes
8–10 slices (1 X 25CM (9IN) CAKE

225g (8oz) plain (all-purpose) flour

125g (4½oz) golden caster (superfine) sugar

135g (5oz) dark brown sugar

1 teaspoon baking powder

1 teaspoon bicarbonate soda (baking soda)

½ teaspoon ground allspice

½ teaspoon ground ginger

½ teaspoon ground cinnamon

½ teaspoon flaky sea salt

90g (3oz) walnuts, roughly chopped

90g (3oz) pitted prunes, roughly chopped

90g (3oz) dried apricots, roughly chopped

120g (4½oz) unsalted butter, melted

200g (7oz) grated carrot (about 2 medium carrots)

zest of 1 large orange

3 eggs

sour cream, to serve

Preheat the oven to 160°C (320°F) and grease and line a 25cm (9in) round cake tin (pan).

Combine the flour, sugars, baking powder, bicarbonate soda, spices, salt and walnuts in a large bowl.

In a separate bowl, mix the dried fruit, melted butter, grated carrot, orange zest and eggs. Add the wet mix to the dry one and stir gently to combine.

Pour the mixture into a tin and bake for 40–50 minutes or until a skewer inserted into the centre of the cake comes out almost clean.

Let the cake cool slightly before serving. Enjoy with a big dollop of sour cream.

MUSHROOMS

CHAPTER SIX

MUSHROOMS

Eastern Europeans are passionate mycophiles. Pick one (the Eastern European, not a mushroom) you know at random and ask, and you will probably find yourself immersed in a beautiful story of woodland adventures and foraging in the local forest at the end of summer with family and friends. Perhaps a romantic overstatement, but it is still true that many people in Eastern Europe live in close connection to nature as the abundance of fertile landscapes makes this relationship and the knowledge that it yields a natural part of life. Take the botanically rich meadows of Transylvania, the eco-haven of the Carpathian Mountains that cover the Czech Republic, Hungary, Poland, Romania, Serbia, Slovakia and Ukraine, or the rich woodlands of Belarus that make up almost half of the country's surface.

While the rest of the vegetables featured in this book were imported to Eastern Europe, albeit long ago enough to become indisputable staples, wild mushrooms are the true locals. Growing untamed and abundant in the rich woodland areas, they also come free of charge and require no effort on behalf of humans to grow, the only real effort required is an understanding of the poisonous and edible varieties. Foraging is such an integral part of the culinary culture that it feels wrong to even use the word effort. It is a real family ritual, a core memory for so many, and the knowledge of mushroom foraging is passed down through the DNA. I treasure so many beautiful memories of foraging expeditions with my grandpa in the early autumn, all of which would conclude with a rather surrealist scene of a bathtub, in their small Soviet-era flat filled with freshly-picked mushrooms. We would kneel by the bathtub and clean off leaves, grass and soil using old toothbrushes. At moments like these, my grandparents' bathroom would fill with the scents of autumnal woodlands and, as I was only a child, I would spend most of the time marvelling at this magical scene rather than actually offering any help. Once cleaned, the mushrooms would make their way into fry-ups, stews, soups, and of course into large glass jars, either dried or to be preserved in a fragrant brine for winter. In this chapter, you will find recipes for all kinds of mushroom dishes, a bite of which is bound to take you on a journey through an Eastern European forest.

MUSHROOMS NATIVE TO EASTERN EUROPE

- Porcini
- Chanterelles
- Honey
- Milkcaps
- Morels

Bulgarian Mushroom and Walnut Pâté

This recipe was recommended to me by a former colleague, Professor Dina Iordanova, a leading scholar of Eastern European cinema from Bulgaria, and a keen foodie. I have taken the liberty of adding the mushrooms to the original walnut pâté, and am very delighted with that decision.

Makes 350g (12oz)

- 20g (¾oz) dried wild mushrooms
- 1 tablespoon olive oil, plus extra for the pâté
- 1 onion, peeled and thinly sliced
- 200g (7oz) mushrooms, roughly chopped
- 1 teaspoon finely chopped thyme leaves
- 4 tablespoons crème fraîche (optional)
- 85–100g (3–3½oz) walnuts
- 1–2 garlic cloves, finely chopped
- salt and black pepper, to taste
- crusty bread, to serve

Soak the dried mushrooms in boiling water, then drain and clean off the grit. Chop finely.

Heat the oil in a frying pan and fry the onion with a pinch of salt over a medium heat for 8–10 minutes.

Add the chopped wild mushrooms, fresh mushrooms and thyme and cook for another 8–10 minutes. Season with salt and pepper. You can also add the crème fraîche here, if using.

Place the walnuts and garlic in a food processor and add about a third of the mushroom mixture to start with, blending until you have a smooth consistency. Keep adding more mushrooms if the texture is too runny. If the mixture is too stiff, add a splash of water and 1–2 tablespoons olive oil.

Season with salt and pepper to taste, and have a fresh crusty baguette ready to dig in.

Tabani – Udmurt Sourdough Pancakes with Mushrooms

This is another fascinating recipe from the Udmurt people, an ethnic group close to the Finns and the Hungarians, who reside in the Eastern European side of the Ural Mountains (as well as in parts of Ukraine, Estonia and Kazakhstan). Tabani are a culinary classic, usually prepared for celebratory weekend breakfasts. Made with a sourdough starter, they are either served plain, smothered in butter, or with various toppings, such as mushrooms, and are always served with a side of *zyret*, a sort of a béchamel dipping sauce. While traditionally these were baked in a cast-iron pan inside a wood-fired oven, called *pech',* these days *tabani* can be made on a stovetop in any frying pan. I have to admit, I had not come across this dish until now, and I absolutely love its unique yet familiar combination of sour pancakes, earthy mushrooms and a creamy sauce.

You'll need to start this recipe the day before as the sourdough starter needs time to develop. All the elements to the recipe can be done in advance, so you can simply finish the batter and cook the pancakes in the morning.

Makes 8–10

FOR THE BATTER

450ml (15fl oz) whole milk

2 tablespoon caster (superfine) sugar

1 teaspoon fast-action dried yeast

230g (8½oz) plain (all-purpose) flour

1 teaspoon salt

FOR THE MUSHROOMS

25g (1oz) salted butter

1 onion or 2 shallots, finely diced

200g (7oz) white button mushrooms, roughly chopped

2 garlic cloves, finely grated

salt and black pepper to taste

FOR THE ZYRET DIPPING SAUCE

300ml (10fl oz) whole milk

2 tablespoons plain (all-purpose) flour

pinch of salt

pinch of sugar

50g (1¾oz) butter, plus extra for frying and greasing

fresh parsley or dill to serve (optional)

Make the sourdough starter by mixing milk, sugar and yeast in a small bowl. Whisk in half the flour until smooth and leave to rest for 8 hours or overnight.

Now to cook the mushrooms. Melt the butter in a frying pan over a low heat, add the onion with a pinch of salt and cook for 10 minutes until softened. Stir in the mushrooms and garlic, season with salt and pepper and cook for a further 10–15 minutes. Set aside.

To make the *zyret,* pour the milk into a saucepan, reserving a couple of tablespoons in a small bowl. Add the flour to the bowl and whisk until smooth. Heat the pan with the milk over a low heat, tip in the flour mixture, add the salt and sugar, and warm it up stirring constantly without allowing it to come to the boil. When the mixture is hot and starts to thicken, take off the heat and stir in the butter. Leave to cool until serving.

To finish the pancakes, add the remaining flour and salt to the sourdough starter, mix well, then leave to rest for 40 minutes.

Melt a knob of butter in a cast-iron frying pan (or one that you'd usually use to make pancakes) and pour in a ladle of the batter. Once bubbles start to appear, add 2 tablespoons of filling across the pancake while the batter is still wet and let the mix cook through. Carefully flip the pancake and cook for a minute on the other side. Set aside on a plate and grease with butter. Continue with the rest of the batter and mushrooms, stacking the finished pancakes with a little knob of butter between each one.

Serve with the dipping sauce, and you can of course add some fresh parsley or dill on top.

Mushroom and Potato Fry-Up

I am delighted to share this recipe from food writer, Anastasia Zolotarev, which revives so many beautiful mushroom memories of my own. Anastasia comes from a Belarussian-Ukrainian family, who immigrated to Australia when she was five. As an adult, Anastasia was drawn to explore her rich Eastern European heritage through food. Her childhood memories, like my own, are filled with beautiful woodlands where mushroom foraging was nothing short of a sacred family ritual, cherished and shared by many generations. Those moments, as Anastaisa puts it, simply 'feel so good for the soul!'. This dish is something that her family (and mine) would cook following a trip to the woods.

Serves
4

60–70g (2–2½ oz) butter

1kg (2lb 4oz) potatoes, peeled and cut into matchsticks

1 onion, thinly sliced

800g (1lb 12oz) white button or chestnut (cremini) mushrooms, roughly chopped

60–70g (2–2½ oz) butter

Melt 15g (½oz) of the butter in a large lidded frying pan over a medium high heat, then add the potatoes, spread them out evenly and cook, uncovered and undisturbed, until the first golden crisp appears. Then, using a broad spatula, flip the potatoes over and cook on the other side. Try to resist the urge to mix and cook for a further 8–10 minutes.

Reduce heat to medium, add another 15g (½oz) of butter and season with salt. Cover with the lid and cook for a further 20–30 minutes, stirring very gently and very occasionally.

Melt another 15g (½oz) of butter in another pan over a medium-high heat and fry the onion with a pinch of salt for 10 minutes. Add the mushrooms and the remaining butter and increase the heat to high. Cook for 8 minutes until crispy and golden. Add salt and pepper, then take off the heat.

In the last 3 minutes of the potato cooking, add everything into the potato pan. Gently stir. Add more salt and pepper to taste.

The dish is so good in its simplicity that it needs no further additions, but you could also serve it with a dollop of sour cream, freshly chopped parsley and a slice of dark rye bread.

Matzah Brei with Mushrooms

It is almost impossible to put into words the joy I experience when eating matzah. It is something I don't do often, purposefully, so as not to spoil the specialness of the moment. Perhaps it is also an unconscious homage to how my family used to eat it back in the Soviet days – infrequently, on special occasions, almost as a secret pleasure. Matzah needs no introduction, as this simplest of wheat crackers is consumed far and wide around the world. However, as far as I know, cooking with matzah is an exclusively Jewish affair. My Ukrainain-Jewish great-grandmother, Rosalia, used to receive boxes of matzah occasionally from her Moscow-based cousin back in the 1980s, and would always make me the most delicious omelette with it. I learnt later that the omelette is an absolute staple of Ashkenazi cuisine, known as *brei*. It was exceptionally special to make *brei* for my daughter not so long ago and revisit the flavour as if for the first time with her. To my delight, she loved it! *Brei* can be made in the most basic way by simply soaking matzah in milk and then adding it to beaten eggs before frying, or you can add extra ingredients like onion, mushrooms or sauerkraut. In some Ashkenazi communities, it is eaten with sugar and cinnamon. I am definitely in the savoury *brei* camp and this recipe is my favourite go-to option (you can even lose the mushrooms and just enjoy the sweet, buttery, caramelised onions).

Serves
2

- 3 matzah sheets, broken into small pieces
- 50ml (1¾fl oz) whole milk
- vegetable oil, for frying
- 1 onion, thinly sliced
- pinch of sugar
- 20g (¾oz) butter
- 200g (7oz) white button or chestnut (cremini) mushrooms, thinly sliced
- 5 eggs, beaten
- salt and black pepper, to taste

Crush the matzah sheets roughly with your hands into a bowl, thenpour over the milk. Let it soak while you prepare the rest.

Heat the oil in a lidded frying pan and add the onion along with a pinch of salt and the sugar. Allow to sweat gently over a medium heat for 15–20 minutes, until softened. Towards the end of the cooking time, add the butter. Stir through the mushrooms, and cook for another 8 minutes.

In a separate bowl, beat the eggs with a pinch of salt, then add the soaked matzah and soaking milk.

Pour the mixture into the pan, gently stir to incorporate the ingredients and cook, covered, over gentle heat for 5–8 minutes until the middle is cooked through. Serve with plenty of black pepper.

Baba's Mushroom Soup

Mushroom soups are a type of Eastern European soul food, with a handful of key ingredients that are then dressed differently to create a multitude of variations. Here is a mother recipe that is at the heart of many Eastern European soups, or rather a 'grandmother recipe', as that's what the word *baba* means in many Slavic languages.

This soup tastes even better when given some time to infuse (overnight if you can). You can also add some cooked buckwheat noodles, some vermicelli or Matzo balls for an extra bite.

Serves
4

vegetable oil, for frying

1 onion, diced

1 large carrot, peeled and grated

2 teaspoons dried dill

400g (14oz) chestnut (cremini) mushrooms (or a mix of mushrooms), roughly chopped

1.5 litres (51fl oz/6 cups) vegetable or chicken stock

1 bay leaf

4 potatoes, peeled and diced

4 tablespoons chopped fresh dill, plus extra to serve

salt and black pepper to taste

sour cream to serve

Heat the oil in a large saucepan and fry the onion, carrot and the dill with a pinch of salt over a medium heat for 8 minutes. Add the mushrooms, season with a bit more salt, and fry for 5–8 minutes until the mushrooms have softened and released their deep, dark liquid.

Next, add the stock and bay leaf, season to taste, bring to the boil and then add the potatoes. Simmer for 10–15 minutes until the potatoes are cooked. Take off heat and add the dill.

When you are ready for the soup and it is ready for you, serve with plenty of black pepper, a generous handful of fresh dill and a dollop of sour cream.

Hot and Sour Mushroom Soup

This soup is a love child of *krupnik* and *zupa ogórkowa*, the two classics from Ukraine and Poland. The natural sweetness of mushrooms enters into dialogue with the sharp tang of the gherkins, while the heartiness of the soup is provided by the grains (*krupa*), either pearl barley or buckwheat. In some ways, this soup can be seen as a vegan counterpart to the duck soup that follows next, but you can add some meat protein here such as smoked pancetta, if you like, just add it to the frying pan together with the onion and carrots.

Serves
4

- 20g (¾oz) dried wild mushrooms
- 150g (5½oz) pearl barley or buckwheat
- 1 bay leaf
- 2 litres (68fl oz/8 cups) vegetable or chicken stock
- vegetable oil, for frying
- 1 onion, diced
- 1 carrot, peeled and grated
- 1 teaspoon dried dill
- 250g (9oz) chestnut (cremini) mushrooms
- 2 tablespoons tomato purée (paste)
- 1 teaspoon sugar
- 1 tablespoon chilli sauce (such as Sriracha) or ½ teaspoon dried chilli (hot pepper) flakes
- 2–4 large pickled gherkins, grated
- 2 large potatoes, peeled and diced
- 2 tablespoons chopped fresh dill
- 1 tablespoon sour cream per plate to serve (optional)

Soak the wild mushrooms in a bowl of hot water for 30 minutes.

Rinse the pearl barley or buckwheat under water well, then drain and place in a large saucepan with the bay leaf and the stock. Bring to a simmer and cook for 30 minutes if using pearl barley or 10 minutes for buckwheat.

In the meantime, heat a little oil in a frying pan. Add the onion and carrot, a pinch of salt and the dried dill. Fry for 15 minutes over medium heat, until the vegetables soften.

Strain the mushrooms through a fine sieve, reserving the liquid but discarding any grit. Roughly chop all the mushrooms (wild and fresh), and add to the frying pan.

Next, add the tomato purée, sugar, chilli sauce, gherkins and mushroom soaking liquid and cook for another 5 minutes. Taste for seasoning and adjust to your liking.

Tip the contents of the pan into a large saucepan, add the potatoes and simmer for 10–15 minutes, until the potatoes are cooked.

Add the dill, take off the heat, cover the pan and let the soup sit for 30 minutes (if you can). As with any Eastern European sour soup, this will taste phenomenal after a night in the fridge.

Duck Soup with Wild Mushrooms and Sauerkraut

This dish does not have an exact location of origin within Eastern Europe, but is rather a riff on various flavours and ingredients, which make a perfect sense to an Eastern European palette. A rich duck broth is complemented by the deep, woody quality of the wild mushrooms and offset with the tang of the sauerkraut. Undoubtedly a late-autumn (fall)/winter dish, it was initially conjured up as a solution for the Christmas leftovers, yet is worth making from scratch at any point during the cooler season.

Serves
4

FOR THE BROTH

2 duck legs

1 tablespoon black peppercorns

1 tablespoon sea salt flakes

1 tablespoon fennel seeds

1 tablespoon coriander seeds

3 bay leaves

1 onion, skin on and washed, cut in half

1 carrot, skin on and washed, cut in half

2 celery sticks

4 garlic cloves, peeled and smashed

a small bunch of parsley stalks

FOR THE SOUP

50g (1¾oz) dried wild mushrooms

vegetable oil, for frying

1 onion, finely diced

1 carrot, peeled and grated

2 potatoes, peeled and diced

100g (3½oz) Classic Sauerkraut (see page 184) or shop-bought

salt and black pepper, to taste

a handful of chopped fresh dill, to serve

To make the stock, place all the ingredients in a large saucepan along with 2 litres (68fl oz/8 cups) water, bring to the boil, then lower the heat and simmer for 2 hours. You might need to skim off the residue from the top a few times and top up with an additional 500ml (2 cups) water if the liquid evaporates too much.

Once the broth is ready, take out the duck legs, pick the meat off the bones into a bowl and set aside. Discard the skin and bones.

Soak the wild mushrooms in a bowl of hot water for 30 minutes, then strain through a fine sieve, reserving the liquid but discarding any grit. Roughly chop the mushrooms and set aside.

Strain the broth through a fine sieve or muslin (cheesecloth), discarding all the vegetables and spices. Return to the pot.

Heat a little oil in a frying pan and add the onion and carrot with a pinch of salt. Fry for 8–10 minutes or until golden and softened. Add the mushrooms and fry for a further 6–8 minutes.

Tip the contents of the pan into the broth, making sure to rinse out the vegetable pan with a ladleful of the broth to scrape out the delicious caramelised bits. Add the mushroom soaking liquid. Bring the soup to the boil, then reduce the heat and add the potatoes and the sauerkraut. Simmer for 10 minutes, until the potatoes are almost tender. At this point, add the duck to the soup and cook for another 5 minutes to warm through. Switch off the heat and let sit for 30 minutes.

Serve with a generous sprinkling of fresh dill and a crack of black pepper.

Mushroom and Beef Zrazy

Zrazy is another culinary phenomenon that has changed with time and geographic regions. These are generally considered to have originated in the Polish-Lithuanian Commonwealth as little roulades of meat with vegetables stewed in a mushroom sauce. However, the dish changed its essence a little, presumably in the absence of the perfect cuts of meat, during the less prosperous times (i.e. the Socialist rule). These types of *zrazy* are made of minced (ground) meat encasing various vegetarian fillings – mushrooms being the most popular one – turning the dish into patties. They would be served with a creamy mushroom sauce and a side of mashed potatoes.

Makes
8–10

vegetable oil, for frying

1 small onion, thinly sliced

250g (9oz) white button or chestnut (cremini) mushrooms, finely diced or grated

25g (1oz) mixed parsley and dill, finely chopped

1 hard-boiled egg, grated

1 egg, lightly beaten

400g (14oz) minced (ground) beef

2–3 garlic cloves, finely chopped

Dijon mustard (optional)

salt and black pepper to taste

gherkins, to serve

Fry the onion in a frying pan with a little oil and a pinch of salt for 8 minutes over a medium heat, or until softened. Add the mushrooms and cook for a further 8–10 minutes.

Take off the heat, add the parsley, dill and the grated hard-boiled egg. Mix thoroughly. Let it cool down a little before handling.

In a bowl, mix the beef mince with garlic and raw egg, and season generously with salt and pepper.

To shape the *zrazy*, place 2 tablespoons of the meat mixture onto a sheet of baking paper and spread it into a large disc. Spread ½ teaspoon of mustard over it, if using. Place a tablespoon of the mushroom mix in the middle and close the edges as if forming a ball, so that the filling is entirely encased. Flatten the ball gently to create a burger patty shape and repeat until you run out of the filling and the meat.

Heat enough oil in a frying pan for shallow-frying over a medium heat. Add the *zrazy*, in batches, and fry for 4–5 minutes each. Remove and drain on paper towels. Serve with mashed potato or a side of gherkins and ferments.

Pierekaczewnik – a Lipka Tatar Snail Pie

There is a restaurant in the Polish village of Kruszyniany, near Bialystok, called The Tatar Yurt that serves the most beautiful homestyle Tatar food. On their menu, you can find an array of dishes both common in post-Socialist culinary culture as well as unique ones to the cuisine of the Tatar community from the north-east of Poland and the neighbouring parts of Lithuania and Belarus, also known as the Lipka Tatars. This dish is one of the latter, and a big hit with customers. It is a real labour of love and is generally prepared for celebratory meals, traditionally weighing up to 3kg (6lb 10oz). The pie, not too dissimilar to the Austro-Hungarian strudel or the South-Eastern European snail pies, is made out of layers of paper-thin dough that are doused in butter and stuffed with either meat and vegetable filling or a sweet filling of twarog, apples and dried fruit. Here I offer a modified (simpler and lighter) version using ready-made filo pastry and a filling of mushrooms and potatoes. If you have any leftover roast meat, it would be a perfect addition to the filling. Serve hot with some slaw and sour cream (of course).

Serves
6–8

- 50g (1¾oz) dried wild mushrooms
- vegetable oil, for frying and greasing
- 2 onions, diced
- 150g (5½oz) butter
- 400g (14oz) white button or chestnut (cremini) mushrooms, roughly chopped
- 400g (14oz) potatoes, peeled and cubed
- 2 bay leaves
- 1 small bunch of dill, finely chopped
- salt and black pepper, to taste
- 1 x packet of ready-to-use filo pastry (270–300g/9½–10oz/ 7–8 sheets)

In a small bowl, soak the dried mushrooms in 100ml (3½fl oz) just-boiled water.

Heat a little oil in a frying pan and fry the onions with a pinch of salt over a medium heat for 8 minutes. Meanwhile, drain the mushrooms, reserving the liquid and discarding any grit. Chop the mushrooms and add them to the pan along with the fresh mushrooms and 50g (1¾oz) of the butter. Let them cook for 5–8 minutes, until their liquid is released, then add the potatoes, bay leaves and mushroom soaking liquid. Bring to a simmer and cook for a further 10–15 minutes until the liquid has been absorbed. Season generously with salt and pepper, and add the finely chopped dill. Take off the heat and let the filling cool while you prepare the dough.

Preheat the oven to 200°C (400°F) and grease a medium-size tin with oil. Melt the remaining 100g (3½oz) butter. Have a bowl with a pastry brush and the melted butter at the ready as you lay out two sheets of filo on a clean, dry surface so that they overlap in the middle lengthwise; you are looking to create one large rectangular sheet. Generously brush the filo sheet with butter, then layer the next two sheets on top in the same way. Brush with butter and repeat with the rest of the pastry.

When the filling is cool enough to handle, spread it out evenly across the entire surface of the pastry and roll into a large cigar shape. Then, tucking one end in, roll the cigar into a snail shape. Brush with the remaining butter all over and carefully place the snail into the prepared tin.

Bake for 45 minutes on the middle shelf of the oven, until crispy and golden brown. Remove and let cool a little on a wire rack, slicing through the middle like you would with a pizza to serve.

Mushroom and Rice Stuffed Peppers in Sour Cream Sauce

While this dish is common throughout Eastern Europe, one look at the ingredients will tell you that it originated in the southern parts of the region that used to be under the control of the Ottoman Empire, such as Bulgaria, Hungary, Romania, Moldova and Southern Ukraine. Stuffed peppers are a staple of Turkish cuisine, and the former Ottoman-controlled countries of Eastern Europe have created variations to make this dish their own. Traditionally made with meat, these mushroom-filled peppers in no way pale in comparison.

Serves
4

8 (bell) peppers

FOR THE FILLING

100g (3½oz) white rice

vegetable oil, for frying

1 onion, diced

1 carrot, peeled and grated

25g (1oz) parsley, finely chopped

2 garlic cloves

200g (7oz) chestnut (cremini) mushrooms, chopped

50g (1¾oz) pine nuts, toasted

FOR THE SAUCE

250g (9oz/1 cup) passata (sieved tomatoes)

1 teaspoon soft brown sugar

250ml (9fl oz/1 cup) vegetable stock

250g (9oz/1 cup) sour cream

salt and black pepper, to taste

handful of parsley or dill, to serve

Slice the tops off the peppers and reserve them, then remove and discard the seeds. Set aside.

Parboil the rice (check the packet instructions and halve the time).

Heat the oil in a frying pan and fry the onion and carrot with a pinch of salt over a medium heat for 10 minutes. Add the parsley, garlic and mushrooms and cook for another 10 minutes.

Mix in the pine nuts and the parboiled rice, generously season with salt and pepper.

Make the sauce by heating the passata with the sugar, salt and pepper and stock in a saucepan. Once steaming hot, take off the heat and mix in the sour cream. Adjust the seasoning to your liking.

Preheat the oven to 200°C (400°F).

Stuff the peppers with the mushroom and rice mixture. Snuggle them tightly upright into an ovenproof casserole (Dutch oven) or baking dish. Pour over the sauce, making sure a little gets inside each pepper. Place the tops back onto the peppers like lids, cover the casserole (if using a baking dish cover with foil) and bake in the oven for 25 minutes. Carefully remove the casserole lid (or foil) and cook uncovered for another 10 minutes.

Serve with a sprinkle of dill or parsley and a chunky slice of bread to mop up the sauce.

Rosie's Buckwheat Stir-Fry with Mushrooms, Pancetta and Kimchi

I simply could not exclude this recipe invented by my four-year-old daughter. I was pregnant with her when I wrote my first cookbook, so it felt particularly special having her next to me in the kitchen when I was testing recipes for this book. Our culinary explorations do not end when we leave the kitchen, and we often play various food-themed games at bathtime, using bath-bubbles and other non-edible objects as gastronomic stand-ins. On one such occasion, Rosie conjured up a dish of buckwheat with bacon, mushrooms and kimchi, which was a genuine lightbulb moment for me. These ingredients indeed make perfect sense together and, with the exception of kimchi, are undoubtedly Eastern European in their essence. She felt so proud hearing that her idea is good enough to be included in the book. So here it is, my daughter's recipe-writing debut! You can also add a fried egg on top to turn this into a luscious weekend brunch dish.

Serves
4

400g (14oz) Eastern European buckwheat (*grechka* or *kasza*)

top-quality, unrefined sunflower oil, to drizzle

50g (1¾oz) diced pancetta (optional)

2 onions, peeled and diced

20g (¾oz) salted butter (optional, if not using bacon)

400g (14oz) chestnut (cremini) mushrooms, diced

4 garlic cloves, finely chopped

100g (3½oz) kimchi (or plain sauerkraut – shop-bought or see page 184)

4 tablespoons finely chopped dill or parsley

Cook the buckwheat according to the packet instructions, then drain, stir in a little sunflower oil and set aside.

Fry the pancetta (if using) and the onions with a pinch of salt in a large saucepan or casserole (Dutch oven) over a medium high heat for 10 minutes. If omitting the pancetta, add the butter. Add the mushrooms, garlic and a pinch of salt, and cook, covered, over medium heat for 8–10 minutes.

Once the mushrooms release their juices, add the buckwheat and the kimchi. Stir thoroughly for 2–4 minutes for all the ingredients and flavours to incorporate.

Sprinkle with fresh herbs and drizzle with a little sunflower oil before serving.

Hungarian Mushroom Paprikash Stew

An absolute classic of Hungarian cuisine, this dish, together with goulsash soup (*gulyás leves*) and *pörkölt* stew, are my top contenders for the ultimate comfort food in autumn and winter. While *pörkölt* is a rich stew of beef in a smoky tomato sauce, a paprikash stew is thickened with sour cream, richly spiced with smoked paprika and always served with a side of noodles, potatoes or *galuska* dumplings. Most commonly made with chicken, here is an equally popular vegetarian alternative using mushrooms. The flavour of paprika is essential to this dish, just as it is to so many dishes of the Hungarian repertoire. It is astonishing to think that paprika was only introduced to Hungary with the Ottoman occupation in the 16th century and not used in cooking until the 1800s.

Serves
4

vegetable oil, for frying

1 onion, thinly sliced

1 red (bell) pepper, cored, deseeded and thinly sliced

800g (1lb 12oz) white button or chestnut (cremini) mushrooms, thinly sliced

2 tablespoons smoked paprika or 1½ tablespoons sweet paprika and ½ tablespoon hot paprika

2 teaspoons dried marjoram

200g (7oz) sour cream or crème fraîche

1 tablespoon finely chopped parsley

salt and black pepper to taste

cooked pasta, such as pappardelle, to serve

Heat up some vegetable oil in a casserole (Dutch oven) or heavy-based lidded frying pan. Add the onion and red pepper with a pinch of salt and cook, covered, over a medium heat for 15 minutes until soft. Add the mushrooms, with another pinch of salt, and cook for 10 minutes, stirring occasionally, until the mushrooms release their juices.

Lower the heat, add the paprika and marjoram, and cook for 5 minutes. Add the sour cream and stir well to let the vegetable juices mix with the cream. Adjust the seasoning, adding some pepper. Simmer gently on the lowest heat, without boiling, for 2–3 minutes. Take the pan off the heat, stir in the parsley and let rest for a little before serving with a side of pappardelle.

PICKLES AND FERMENTS

CHAPTER SEVEN

PICKLES AND FERMENTS

Fermented food is the stuff of life in Eastern Europe. It is one of the oldest forms of 'cooking' and preserving food in many parts of the region, one that dates back at least to the 10th century. It encapsulates the food philosophy that I depict in the introduction perhaps better than any other dish or cooking technique in this book. By opening a jar of fermented food we gain access to the culinary, the cultural and the political history of Eastern Europe. Those jars of preserved seasonal glut accompany generation upon generation of Eastern Europeans throughout their lives and through their region's turbulent histories. Those jars kept my grandfather company when he was hiding in the cellar of a neighbour's house, as a five-year-old Jewish boy in Nazi-occupied Ukraine in the early 1940s. And those were the jars I saw in a picture a friend posted online of a bomb shelter in Kharkiv of 2022: a concrete box of basement with some mattresses thrown on the floor and an entire wall of jars filled with sauerkraut, fermented tomatoes and cucumbers. I didn't know what it was like to hide in a shelter during a bombing, but I knew exactly what those fermented vegetables tasted like. And for a moment that taste, which I could recall instantly, brought me viscerally close to the people in the picture.

Of course, fermented food is not always associated with profound historical traumas but is rather an essential part of life; of people's celebratory and everyday tables, the source of vital nutrients and of powerful flavours.

This chapter offers an exciting range of fermented and pickled vegetables, starting with the classic fermented cabbage with carrots, caraway and bay leaf – a building block of many delicious recipes – working our way up to more experimental flavours. There are a million and one ways to serve ferments and pickles – on their own, lightly dressed with high-quality sunflower or rapeseed oil, as a side to many main courses, in salads, sandwiches, stews and soups. I hope this book offers plenty of recipes to let you experience the wonder of preserved foods in their full glory.

Classic Sauerkraut

Makes
1 x 1 litre jar (34FL OZ/4 CUPS)

- 1 large white cabbage
- 2 large carrots
- 2 tablespoons fine sea salt
- 1 teaspoon toasted caraway seeds (optional)
- 4 bay leaves

Remove the outer leaves of the cabbage and set aside. Quarter and thinly slice the cabbage using a mandoline or a sharp knife. Peel and grate the carrots. Place the cabbage and carrots in a large mixing bowl and sprinkle with the salt. Add the caraway seeds if using. Massage the salt into the vegetables for about 15–20 minutes, taking breaks if preferred.

Mix the bay leaves through the vegetables. You are now ready to pack the jar.

'MASTER' METHOD FOR FERMENTS

Sterlise your jar by washing it in warm soapy water, then rinse, drain, place on a baking tray and dry in an oven pre-heated to 160°C (350°F) for 15 minutes.

Pack in the cabbage as tightly as you can. You don't want any air pockets forming as this will be a breeding ground for harmful bacteria. Using your fist or the end of a rolling pin will do the trick. Make sure to leave about 3cm (1¼in) space before the rim of the jar, as the cabbage will gradually expand, resulting in a lot of spillage.

When you have completed the final layer, place the reserved outer cabbage leaves on top, and press down with something heavy like a stone or a freezer bag filled with water.

Place the jar into a bowl or on top of a plate, to catch any of the escaping brine. The cabbage will make its magical transformation into sauerkraut in 7–14 days (keep it out of direct sunlight), depending on the room temperature. Make sure you check in on it every day, opening the jar, and pressing the cabbage back into the brine if needed.

At this point you can transfer it to the fridge to slow down the fermentation process or, for a more vintage quality, leave the jar out on the shelf and it will mature gracefully.

Sauerkraut with Cranberries

Makes
1 x 1 litre jar (34FL OZ/4 CUPS)

- 1 large white cabbage
- 400g (14oz) fresh cranberries, cut in half
- 2 tablespoons fine sea salt
- 1 tablespoon caster (superfine) sugar
- 1 large bunch of dill, finely chopped

Remove the outer leaves of the cabbage, and set aside. Quarter and thinly slice the cabbage using a mandoline or a sharp knife. Place in a large mixing bowl with salt. Massage the salt into the cabbage for about 10–15 minutes, taking breaks if preferred.

Add the sliced cranberries, sugar and dill, and give it a thorough mix, incorporating all elements together.

Pack the mixture into a jar following the 'master method' on page 184.

Sauerkraut with Apple and Orange

Makes
1 x 1 litre jar (34FL OZ/4 CUPS)

- 1 large white cabbage
- 2 tablespoons fine sea salt
- 1 teaspoon toasted fennel seeds
- 2 green apples
- 1 large orange
- 1 small bunch of dill, chopped

Remove the outer leaves of the cabbage, and set aside. Quarter and thinly slice the cabbage using a mandoline or a sharp knife. Place in a large mixing bowl with the salt. Massage the salt into the cabbage for about 10–15 minutes, taking breaks if preferred.

Core and thinly slice the apples. Zest and juice the orange.

Add the apple slices, orange zest and juice and chopped dill into the bowl with the cabbage, and give it a thorough mix.

Pack the mixture into a jar following the 'master method' on page 184.

Fermented Slaw

Makes
1 x 1 litre jar (34FL OZ/4 CUPS)

- ½ white cabbage, shredded
- 1 large cucumber, thinly sliced
- 1 large carrots, peeled and grated
- 1 large red (bell) pepper, thinly sliced
- 2 tablespoons fine sea salt
- 1 tablespoon allspice berries
- 1 teaspoon dried dill
- 2 bay leaves

Place the thinly sliced and grated vegetables in a large bowl with the salt and massage for 10 minutes or so, taking breaks. Add the allspice berries, dill and bay leaves, and give it another good mix.

Pack the mixture into a jar following the 'master method' on page 184.

Red Cabbage, Beetroot and Horseradish Sauerkraut

Makes
1 x 1 litre jar (34FL OZ/4 CUPS)

1 medium red cabbage
2 tablespoons fine sea salt
2 large beetroots (beets)
2 thumbs of fresh horseradish
1 large bunch of dill, chopped
2 tablespoons clear honey

Make sure to wear some gloves for this recipe.

Remove the outer leaves of the cabbage, and set aside. Quarter and thinly slice the cabbage using a mandoline or a sharp knife. Set aside in a bowl with the salt.

Peel and grate the beetroots and the horseradish, then add to the bowl with the cabbage, along with the dill. Massage for 10 minutes, taking breaks if preferred. Add the honey and give it another thorough mix.

Pack the mixture into a jar following the 'master method' on page 184.

Red Cabbage, Beetroot, Bay Leaf and Blackberry Sauerkraut

Makes
1 x 1 litre jar (34FL OZ/4 CUPS)

1 medium or ½ large red cabbage
2 tablespoons fine sea salt
1 tablespoon soft brown sugar
2 medium beetroots (beets)
250g (9oz) blackberries, halved
4 bay leaves

Make sure to wear gloves for this recipe.

Remove the outer leaves of the cabbage and set aside. Quarter and thinly slice the cabbage using a mandoline or a sharp knife. Set aside in a bowl with the salt and sugar.

Peel and grate the beetroots and add to the bowl with the cabbage. Give both a good massage for 10 minutes, taking breaks if preferred.

Add the blackberries and bay leaves to the bowl. Give everything a thorough mix.

Pack the mixture into a jar following the 'master method' on page 184. When packing the jar be mindful not to squeeze or bash the berries too much.

THE MAGIC OF FERMENTED FOODS!

It is an honour to share this story from a fellow food writer of Jewish-Ukrainian lineage, Anna Kharzeeva. It belongs to her great-grandmother, Munya Izrailevna Maisil, and recalls an evening in Kyiv during the aftermath of the Revolution in the early 1920s.

'During the civil war, which lasted several years after the Revolution, we lived in Kyiv and the government changed eight times in a very short space of time. My family [parents and six siblings] had guests over – imagine how many people there were with each of us bringing a friend or two! We were playing games and missed the curfew, which meant everyone had to stay overnight. My mother was terrified as there was no food in the house. So my friend and I went to the basement and got some potatoes, some sour cabbage, pickled cucumbers and tomatoes out of wooden barrels, and set a beautiful table with just the four types of food. We still had beautiful plates and cutlery, so it looked very formal. I went into the living room and said, "I'd like to invite everyone to the dining room." My mother looked terrified, as she knew there was no food in the house. Everyone was stunned at the dinner we'd scraped together.'

Fermented Cabbage Leaves

Kapusta

Makes
1 x 3 litre jar (101FL OZ/12 CUPS)

1 white cabbage (800g–1kg/1lb 12oz–2lb 4oz)

40g (1½oz) fine sea salt

10g (¼oz) caster (superfine) sugar

1 tablespoon black peppercorns or allspice berries

4 bay leaves

Prepare the cabbage leaves by carefully cutting out the cabbage core and separating as many leaves as you possibly can without tearing. You might need to continue cutting the core out as you get towards the middle, where the leaves are tighter.

Prepare the salt solution by dissolving the salt and sugar in 2 litres (68fl oz/8 cups) just-boiled water, then let it cool down completely.

Pack the leaves into a sterilised jar, reserving two, add the spices and bay leaves, and pour over the brine. Place the reserved cabbage leaves on top, and press down with something heavy like a stone or a freezer bag filled with water to keep the leaves submerged in the brine. Leave out of direct sunlight at room temperature for 10–14 days.

Make sure you check in on it every day, opening the jar, and pressing the cabbage back into the brine if needed.

At this point, you can transfer it into the fridge to slow down the fermentation process or, for a more vintage quality, leave the jar out on the shelf and it will mature gracefully.

Pickled Red Peppers Stuffed with Cabbage

Makes
1 x 5 litre jar (50FL OZ/6 CUPS)

6 red (bell) peppers

1 small white cabbage (weighing approx. 400g/14oz), shredded

4 carrots, peeled and grated

12 small hot chillies, finely chopped

6–8 garlic cloves, thinly sliced

1 large bunch of fresh parsley (about 50g/1¾oz), roughly chopped

fine sea salt, to taste

FOR THE VINEGAR BRINE

4 bay leaves

1 teaspoon black peppercorns

1 teaspoon coriander seeds

4–6 tablespoons caster (superfine) sugar

1 scant tablespooon salt

450ml (15fl oz) apple cider vinegar or white wine vinegar

First, prepare the peppers. Cut off the tops of the peppers and remove the seeds carefully, keeping the main part intact. Wash and set aside.

Prepare the filling by mixing the cabbage, carrots, chillies, garlic and parsley in a large bowl with enough salt that the slaw is on the edge of being over-seasoned. Stuff each pepper with the cabbage slaw mixture and pack tightly into a jar, sterilised following the method on page 184. (If you are like me, here you'd be wishing your parents exposed you to Lego or Tetris games as a child.)

Next, prepare the vinegar brine. Combine all the ingredients in a large saucepan and add 650ml (22fl oz) water. Bring to a gentle simmer, then take off and let it cool down. Top the jar with the brine, trying not to pour directly into the peppers, then seal the jar and store in a cool place or refrigerate for 3–4 days before tasting. You might want to keep it a little longer to intensify the flavours or less if you prefer a milder-tasting pickle.

Pickled Mushrooms

Makes
1 x 500ml jar (17FL OZ/2 CUPS)

1 shallot, thinly sliced

200g (7oz) white button mushrooms

2 bay leaves

4 cloves

2 garlic cloves, thinly sliced

1 teaspoon fennel seeds or coriander seeds

1 teaspoon black peppercorns

1 heaped teaspoon fine sea salt

1 tablespoon caster (superfine) sugar

150ml (5fl oz) white wine vinegar

Combine all the ingredients in a large saucepan and pour over 150ml (5fl oz) water. Bring to the boil and simmer for 15 minutes. Taste for seasoning and adjust to your liking.

Let it cool down completely before transferring into a sterilised (see page 184) jar.

Keep in the fridge overnight before tasting, then store in the fridge for up to 3 months.

Ingredients that feature in an Eastern European Kitchen

BEETROOT

Unless specified otherwise, please use raw beetroot for all the recipes. To find the freshest bunch possible, buy from a local greengrocer or a food market, where you can get beetroot with leaves, rather than a supermarket. The leaves are a great indicator of the freshness and are a perfect addition to borsch (see pages 64–70) or stew (see page 72).

BUCKWHEAT

Buckwheat is a groat that is used as a grain in the cuisines of the eastern countries of Eastern Europe. Often referred to as *kasha* or *kasza* (which means porridge or cereal) buckwheat usually comes in a roasted form, so this is the type that is used throughout the book. You can buy this kind from any Eastern European shop, and the varieties usually come from Poland or the Baltics. I would not recommend using the raw green buckwheat that is usually sold in health stores, as its texture and flavour are very different to the traditional Eastern European toasted kind.

GHERKINS

Traditionally, most Eastern European dishes that call for gherkins (dill pickles) would use lacto-fermented cucumbers rather than vinegar-pickled ones, however, for convenience, you can opt for any type of pickled cucumber you happen to have in your pantry. If you want to go the extra mile, most Eastern European shops will have a selection of fermented cucumbers, some pre-packaged, others swimming in brine in large crates. Look for labels that say 'sour gherkins'. Or make your own, using my family recipe from my cookbook *Salt &Time*.

KEFIR

Kefir is a fermented milk drink that has gained a lot of popularity in the West in recent years. These days you can buy a bottle of kefir in most supermarkets. But if you can't find any there then head to the nearest Eastern European shop, where you will find a range to choose from. Always opt for the full-fat stuff. And don't confuse it with water kefir, which is a fizzy drink similar to kombucha.

MATZAH (AKA MATZO)

Traditional Jewish Passover crackers, matzah are available in most supermarkets and in all Jewish delicatessens (unless you shop last-minute the day before Seder, as I did this year!). Opt for the traditional large sheets rather than biscuit-sized ones that some commercial brands offer. Matzah sheets are not to be confused with matzo meal or matzah balls.

OILS

Throughout the book I reference the 'special' Eastern European oils which give dishes their unique flavour, such as unrefined cold-pressed sunflower oil, a signature oil of Ukraine and its neighbouring countries. A high-quality rapeseed oil can be used too, as it often is in Polish cooking. These can be found in Eastern European shops (I'd highly recommend finding a premium Ukrainian brand). For all other occasions I use an organic flavourless sunflower oil for frying.

SAUERKRAUT

While I encourage you to make your own fermented cabbage, recipes like stews, soups and stuffing for pies and dumplings work just fine with shop-bought sauerkraut. There are many brands these days from Germany or Poland that offer a decent-quality plain sauerkraut. I'd not worry here about buying a 'live' kraut from a fancy health-food shop as you will be cooking with it, and thus removing all the live bacteria anyway. A simple pasteurised jarred sauerkraut is perfectly acceptable.

SPICES

I hope this list will help you create or expand your collection of Eastern European spices: allspice berries, bay leaf, caraway seeds, coriander seeds, dried herbs (dill, parsley, thyme, lovage), juniper berries, marjoram, smoked paprika (both sweet and hot).

TWAROG CHEESE

Twarog is a type of curdled crumbly soft cheese that is similar to ricotta, only a lot grainier and drier. It can also be compared to quark, farmer's or cottage cheese. In Ukraine, this type of cheese is known as *syr* (the word itself also means 'cheese'), *túró* in Hungary, *tvaroh* in Slovakia and Czechia, *izvara* in Bulgaria, *branza* in Romania and Moldova, *tvorog* in Russia, and *tvarog* in Belarus. You can use any of the above for recipes in this book.

A NOTE ON PORTION SIZES

Many would agree that what makes a meal Eastern European is the size of its portion. Sharing food generously and in abundance is a beautiful feature of the cuisine of the region. So, bearing that in mind, most portion suggestions are on a slightly larger side. And I would love to think of you hosting your own Eastern European gathering, keeping that spirit of generosity alive!

A NOTE ON SALT

Throughout this book, I have used fine sea salt for general seasoning. In some cases I specify sea salt flakes, my preferred brand in the UK being Maldon Sea Salt.

Index

Vegetarian Recipes

MENU SUGGESTIONS

CELEBRATIONS

Herby smetana bed with colourful beets, page 62
A cabbage strudel, page 38
Polish pierogi with sauerkraut and mushrooms, page 115
Kobete – pryazovia Greek meat and potato pie, page 104, with White cabbage slaw, page 26
Beetroot and rye chocolate cake, page 76

COMFORT FOOD

Polish potato and gherkin salad, page 84
Classic beef borsch, page 67,
Hungarian mushroom paprikash stew, page 178
or
Mushroom and beef zrazy, page 170, with Tovchanka – Ukrainian potato and bean mash, page 92
A platter of assorted sauerkraut, pages 184, 186 and 192

SHABBAT DINNER

Knishes – Ashkenazi buns with caramelised carrots and chicken, page 138
Beetroot mayo and prunes dip, page 60
Kreplach – Ashkenazi dumplings in a vegan soup, page 110
Tzimmes – Ashkenazi carrot, beef and prune stew, page 147
Red cabbage, beetroot and horseradish sauerkraut, page 192
Tzimmes carrot cake, page 152

A PICNIC

Pirozhki buns, with cabbage, spring onion and hard-boiled eggs, page 30
Chiboreki – Crimean Tatar flatbreads with lentils and carrots, page 143
Fennel and potato salad with mustard and dill, page 86
Summer potato salad, page 89
Patatnik – Bulgarian potato pie, page 102
Carrot tapenade, page 134
Rye, beetroot and beef meatballs with coriander and gherkins, page 75
Fermented slaw, page 195

BRUNCH

Latkes, page 100, or Potato babka, page 99
Beetroot and egg garlicky mayo spread, page 60
Matzah brei with mushrooms, page 164
Tabani – Udmurt sourdough pancakes with mushrooms, page 160
Carrot, honey and twarog fritters, page 150

A VEGETARIAN FEAST

Taratura – Ukrainian beetroot, gherkin and horseradish salad, page 61
Pearl barley tabbouleh with roasted carrots and walnuts, page 139
Beetroot and kidney bean stew with chard and feta, page 72
Pierrkaczewnik – a Lipka Tatar snail pie, page 173
Pickled mushrooms, page 198
Udmurt dumplings with beetroot and raspberry, page 128

ZAKUSKI PARTY

Cabbage, pea and dill fritters, page 28
Latkes, page 100
Kartoplianyky – Ukrainian potato pasties, page 98
Bulgarian mushroom and walnut pâté, page 158
Spiced beetroot with fried walnuts, page 58
Smoky carrot and red pepper cream cheese, page 136
Fermented slaw, page 189
Pickled red peppers stuffed with cabbage, page 196

SUPPLIERS

The majority of ingredients used in this book are widely available in most supermarkets, but you can source a few specialty ones via the suppliers listed here.

UK

Vadasz Deli
Excellent home-style Eastern European fermented and pickled foods. Available at many UK supermarkets and online.
www.vadaszdeli.co.uk

Good quality unrefined organic sunflower oil.
www.clearspring.co.uk

Excellent range of spices, including all mentioned in the book.
www.spicemountain.co.uk

Eastern European buckwheat
https://www.grechka.co.uk
www.belazu.com

Kefir
Biotiful
Widely available in all major UK supermarkets

RESTAURANTS

These restaurants are all places where you can enjoy authentic Eastern European cuisine.

UK

Bulgarian

Bolyari
290 Green Lanes, London
N13 5TW

Czech and Slovak

Bohemia House
74 West End Lane, West Hampstead, London NW6 2LX
https://bohemiahouse.london

Hungarian

Lake House
83 High Road, London
E18 2QP, UK
https://www.lakehouserestaurant.co.uk

Moldovan

Restaurant Moldova
389-391 Eastern Avenue,
Ilford IG2 6LR
https://restaurantmoldova.co.uk

Polish

Ognisko
55 Exhibition Road,
London SW7 2PG
https://www.ogniskorestaurant.co.uk

Corniluius
1 New River Avenue,
Hornsey, London, N87QD
restaurantcornelius.co.uk

Romanian

Noroc
149 Green Lanes,
Tottenham, London, N13 4SP

Ukrainian

Mriya
275 Old Brompton Road
London SW5 9JA
@mriya_neo_bistro

US

Dacha46
pop ups and online orders
https://www.dacha46.com

Hungarian Pastry Shop
1030 Amsterdam Avenue,
New York 10025-1725

Kachka
960 SE 11th Avenue, Portland,
Oregon 97214
https://www.kachkapdx.com/menus1

Katz Deli
205 E. Houston St., New York,
10002
https://katzsdelicatessen.com

Russ & Daughters Cafe
127 Orchard St., New York, 10002
https://www.russanddaughterscafe.com

Veselka
144 2nd Avenue, New York,
NY 10003
https://veselka.com

Yonah Schimmel's Knish Bakery
137 East Houston Street,
New York, NY 10002
http://www.knishery.com

ABOUT THE AUTHOR

Alissa Timoshkina is a food writer, cook and historian specialising in Eastern European food culture. Born in Siberia, Alissa comes from a family with a rich Eastern European heritage: Ukrainian-Jewish and Polish on her mother's side, and Ukrainian, Russian and Belarussian on her father's side. A recent family DNA test revealed unexpected links to other Eastern European countries (Hungary, Romania, Czechia and the Balkans), rooting her family further into the region. Alissa came to the UK in the late 1990s to study, gaining a PhD in the field of Soviet cinema and Holocaust history from the University of London, where she also worked as a lecturer. However, her love of cooking pulled her away from an academic career, and Alissa launched a supper club and a catering company, KinoVino, in 2015. In 2019 she authored her debut cookbook *Salt & Time: Recipes from a Russian Kitchen*, which was a finalist in two categories at the Guild of Food Writers Awards in the UK and the Julia Child Awards in the USA. Alissa was working on her second cookbook when Russia invaded Ukraine in February 2022. Putting an end to Alissa's book project, the invasion prompted an idea for a global fundraising campaign #CookforUkraine. Since its inception, #CookForUkraine has raised close to £2.5 million ($3.2 million). The project received The Champions of Change Award from World's 50 Best Restaurants, The Editors' Choice Award at the 2022 Observer Food Monthly Awards and The Guild of Food Writers Special Award in 2023.

Alissa lives in North London with her partner and their two children. *Kapusta* is her second book.

@alissatimoshkina
www.alissatimoshkina.com

THANK YOU

This book was an absolute dream come true and I am beyond grateful to the most brilliant commissioning editor, Kajal Mistry, for her faith in my work. Getting a deal without an agent was exceptionally challenging, but Kajal's warmth, generosity and guidance made it all okay in the end!

A huge thanks to the rest of the team at Quadrille. It's been such a pleasure working with you all at various stages of this book: Isabel Gonzalez-Prendergast, Emma Hopkin and Judith Hannam. Thank you, Kate Manwimolruk and Lucy Kingett for your copy editing and proofreading, correcting my 'baby brain' mistakes.

I would probably need another page to express my gratitude to the incredible creative trio –photographer, Laura Edwards, food stylist, Tamara Vos, and prop stylist, Tabitha Hawkins. You have proved once and for all that Eastern European food, and cabbage in particular, are absolutely gorgeous! A big shout out to the wonderful assistants on the shoots: Jo Cowan, Matthew Hague, Phoebe Pearson, Charlotte Whatcott and El Kemp.

A big thank you to Natalia Cummings of @experienceukraineandbeyond for providing beautiful Ukrainian props for the shoot.

I am in absolute awe of the graphic designer Emma Wells (at Nic+Lou). The book cover and each chapter opener will be printed out to grace the walls of my kitchen for years to come!

I am so honoured to include the voices of these brilliant women who have contributed recipes and stories to the book: Anastasia Zolotarev, Polina Chesnokova, Firuza Yusupova, Anna Kharzeeva, and Olga Koutseridi. An additional thank you to Olga for her recipe testing input.

Thank you to other recipe testers: Sharon Browell, Olga Timoshkina and Vera Root. My mom, Olga, and dad, Dmitri, were a huge help at the time of the second shoot, bouncing the baby and lending a hand (sometimes quite literally) whenever needed.

A huge thank you to all these wonderful people who so generously answered my (endless) questions about their native cuisines, shared their family recipes, sent me photos of old cookbooks, and took part in my questionnaire: Dina Iordanova, Ester Pfeiffer, Ola Irnazarow, Zuza Zak, Joana Ptasia, Anna Didynska, Kasia Borowiecka, Małgorzata Burdzy, Dobromila Malinowska, Kamil Tarkowski, Evangeline Harbury, Katia Dukanovic, Ralitsa Dikova, Lusya Galkina, Anna David, Kata Bartos, Zuzana Oswaldova, Veronika Konstiakova, Raluca Micu, Alexandra Antal, Oana Chirila, Roxana Micu, Larisa Viorica Florian, Ana Maria Croitoru, Elena Draghiceanu, Diana Sacalus, Gabriela - Alexandra Tanase, Andrea Grigoroiu, Natalia Aleinova, Natalie Cotrobai, Maryana Dermenzhi, Mariana Paladi, Patricia Arama, Galia Aleshina, Alexandrina Migaevschii, and others (apologies if I've not been able to include every single person).

I am so grateful to the many wonderful food writers who came before me and have been a source of inspiration over the years and especially for this book: Zuza Zak, Irina Georgescu, Olia Hercules, Leah Koenig, Alice Zaslavsky, Darra Goldstein, Anya Von Bremzen, Claudia Roden, Joan Nathan, Michal Korkosz amongst others.

Although we know babies don't come from cabbage, a very special shout out goes to the loveliest Kapusta babies – Freddie, Sona, and Nina – who were with us on the book shoot at various stages of their (gestational) life.

The most special thanks of all goes to my little family unit – Steve, Rosie and Freddie! The youngest member of the team challenged me a bit with extreme morning sickness during the early stages of the book writing and extreme sleep deprivation during the final edits, but I'd not have it any other way. Together we have consumed more cabbage than any average household and I love you all to bits for that! Rosie has been the most brilliant recipe testing assistant not to mention her very own contribution to the book! And Steve, thank you for being there for me through my craziest journey from book and baby n1 to book and baby n2. None of this would have been possible without you!

Quadrille, Penguin Random House UK, One Embassy Gardens, 8 Viaduct Gardens, London SW11 7BW

Quadrille Publishing Limited is part of the Penguin Random House group of companies whose addresses can be found at global.penguinrandomhouse.com

Published by Quadrille in 2025

www.penguin.co.uk

A CIP catalogue record for this book is available from the British Library

ISBN 9781784885854

10 9 8 7 6 5 4 3

Publishing Director Kajal Mistry
Designer Emma Wells, Studio Nic+Lou
Photographer Laura Edwards
Props Stylist Tabitha Hawkins
Food Stylist Tamara Vos
Copy-editor Kate Wanwimolruk
Proofreader Lucy Kingett
Production Manager Sabeena Atchia

Colour reproduction by p2d

Printed in China by C&C Offset Printing Co., Ltd.

The authorised representative in the EEA is Penguin Random House Ireland, Morrison Chambers, 32 Nassau Street, Dublin D02 YH68.

Penguin Random House is committed to a sustainable future for our business, our readers and our planet. This book is made from Forest Stewardship Council® certified paper.